The Great Starvation:
An Irish Holocaust

Seamus Metress, PhD
Anthropology Dept.
University of Toledo

Richard A. Rajner, MA
History Dept.
University of Toledo

American Ireland Education Foundation
PEC
Stony Point, New York

Dedication

Dedicated to the victims of British imperialism and racism in Ireland. May their ghosts and their executioners know that we remember.

Skibbereen[*]

Oh, father dear, I often hear you speak of
    Erin's isle,
Her lofty scenes and valleys green, and her
    mountains rude and wild,
They say she is a lovely land wherein a
    prince might dwell.
Then, why did you abandon it? The reason
    to me tell.

My son I loved my native land with energy
    and pride,
But a blight came over all the land and my
    sheep, my cattle, died;
The rent and taxes were to pay, I could not
    them redeem,
And that's the cruel reason why I left old
    Skibbereen.

---

[*]traditional

It's well do I remember that bleak November
day,
When the bailiff and the landlord came to
drive us all away;
They set the roof on fire with their cursed
English spleen,
And that's another reason that I left old
Skibbereen.

Your mother, too, God rest her soul, lay on
the snowy ground,
She had fainted in her anguishing seeing the
desolation round.
She never rose, but passed away from life to
immortal dream,
And found a cold, white grave, my son, in
our home in old Skibbereen.

And you were only two years old and feeble
was your frame,
I could not leave you with my friends, for
you bore your father's name--
So I wrapt you in my cota mor at the dead of
night unseen.
I heaved a sigh and said good-bye to my
dear old Skibbereen.

Oh, well do I remember the year of '48,
When I rose with comrades brave and true
 to battle against fate.
I was hunted through the hills by slaves who
 served a foreign Queen,
And that's another reason why I left old
 Skibbereen.

Oh, father dear, the day will come when on
 vengeance we call,
And Irish men both stout and tall will rally
 unto the call.
I'll be the man to lead the van beneath the
 flag of green,
And loud and high we'll sound the cry--
 Revenge for Skibbereen.

Illustrated London News

Searching for Potatoes

Ireland and Great Britain

Soup Kitchen

Illustrated London News

Table of Contents

List of Figures

List of Tables

Ireland's Traditional Provinces

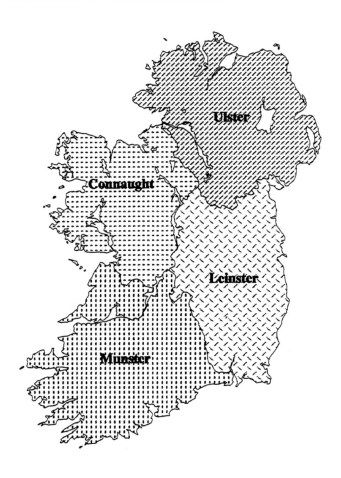

Ireland's 32 Counties

Acknowledgements

We would like to give special thanks to Donna Johnston and Katherine Rajner. Both of these women have given many hours to the project. Donna patiently typed and retyped the manuscript several times and made a seemingly endless series of revisions. And Katherine's editorial critique helped clarify the work as it passed through its many stages.

We would like to thank the American Ireland Education Foundation and its Political Education Committee for publishing this work. The PEC founded by John Finucane in 1975 has been at the forefront of Irish causes for two decades. The Committee has been particularly outspoken on the issues related to the starvation years in Ireland. It has spearheaded an attempt to exact an apology from the British Government for its role in the Great Starvation.

It is also fitting to acknowledge our deceased friend Tom Gallagher the author of <u>Paddys Lament</u>. Tom and other boldly candid individuals and groups, such as the PEC, would not let the British or their Irish collaborators "bury the ghost of the starvation".

We thank Brian Mór O'Baoigill for the use of his sketch on the cover.

Introduction

Ireland's potato failure of the mid-1840s has been variably referred to as "The Great Hunger," "The Great Famine" and "The Great Starvation." One's choice of words to describe this human tragedy has often been determined by political ideology. At the time, most ordinary Irish people called it "An Gorta Mor", or "The Great Hunger", since they were not concerned with ideology but the basic fact that they had no food. Whatever term is used, the Irish potato failure was one of the greatest human ecological disasters in the history of the world.

For Irish landowners and some of their more prosperous tenants and middlemen, the time period was that of "The Great Hunger." Most of the landowners, who lived in Great Britain, were absentee and did not experience first hand the ravages of the potato blight. They, unlike most of their tenants, were not dependent on the potato for their survival. While potatoes rotted in the fields, government officials, British soldiers and the well to do continued to eat a varied diet.

The British call it "The Great Famine." The scarcity of food was blamed on the weather, the potato fungus, God's wrath and, perhaps, most of all, on the Malthusian notion of over-population. The Irish had overbred and there wasn't enough food to feed them all, given the crop failure. However, as Frank O'Connor observed, "Famine is a useful word when you do not wish to use words like 'genocide' and 'extermination'" (1967:133).

These latter terms are philosophically embodied in "The Great Starvation," which we feel is a more accurate portrayal of the time period when Irish peasants starved in the midst of plenty. Wheat, oats, barley, butter, eggs, beef and pork were exported from Ireland in large quantities during the so-called "famine." In fact, during the worst year of the disaster, 1847, in August eight ships left Ireland daily carrying these many basic foodstuffs. The causes of widespread starvation among the Irish peasants were rooted in a colonial system that made them dependent on the potato in the first place. Racist insensitivity toward the plight of the starving masses also played a major role in the death and large-scale emigration which marked this period and the colonial power, Great Britain. The British failed to take swift and comprehensive action in the face of Ireland's disaster.

In recent years there has been an effort to rewrite the history of the Irish Starvation, in order to soften the trauma of the period and downplay the role of the British. This revisionism is especially evident in the tendency to reduce the estimates of the number of deaths related to the starvation. Some have suggested there were far fewer than a million deaths, while other estimates go as low as 250,000, or one out of every forty persons. Even these incorrect estimates are appalling given that they occurred only a short distance from the heart of the most powerful and wealthy empire the world has ever known. We suppose that such an approach is an attempt to lessen the blame that should be placed upon the British or in some sense to veil the magnitude of the tragedy. But as Patrick Campbell concludes in his study of Templecrone in Donegal:

> The horror of the Irish famine is not in the numbers, but in the way they died, because as Francis Forster stated in 1847 when describing death in Templecrone, death by hunger is the most terrible of all deaths: 'So slow yet so certain'. That slow agonizing death of men, women and little children is the real horror and this should be the focus of any study of the Famine (Campbell, 1995).

The revisionist writers contend that there was nothing that any government could have done to ameliorate the situation. They put forth a theory that the British tried to provide relief, but were simply overwhelmed by the logistics of the operation. In the revisionist's view the starvation was the inevitable outcome of demography and the prevalent economic theory of the day. At the same time, especially since renewed hostilities in the Northeast of Ireland, there has been great emphasis on the discontinuity between the past and present in Irish history. For writers such as Roy Foster and others of his ilk, there is nothing in the Irish past that has relevance today. It is as if accurately documenting past injustices, will somehow be used as a weapon by the men and women who espouse the Irish nationalist cause in the current era. Finally, in the opinion of a considerable number of revisionists the period of the Great Starvation was not a significant watershed in the history of Ireland. It was simply an inevitable, but in many ways useful paroxysm in the overall scheme of Irish history.

This short work will be an attempt to analyze "The Great Starvation" from a biocultural or holistic perspective. We will examine the interaction of the biophysical, historical, social, political and economic factors that resulted in the death and forced emigration of so many Irish people. We place the blame squarely upon the shoulders of Britain and its history of oppressive rule in Ireland. The Great

Starvation was an ugly and tragic historical event. It is a massive indictment of British imperialism and a challenge to the moral integrity of British society and culture.

The Great Starvation is difficult to study objectively since the details of the story are so offensive that it cuts to the very soul. Starving people should not become simply objects for study or promoting careers. Those who chronicle or analyze the period must be allowed to show compassion and accept its personal challenge to our humanity.

I
The Background to Starvation

The crop failure and events surrounding it are best analyzed from the broad perspective of biocultural ecology. The biophysical failure was the result of the interaction of the potato blight with unusual climatic conditions. But the human ecological impact was greatly affected by the sociohistorical context in which the biological failure occurred. Biology, geography, history and social structure in the context of 19th century colonialism determined the course of the Irish catastrophe.

The Irish potato failure occurred in the nineteenth century. Its roots, however, are firmly embedded in the exploitation of Ireland to serve the needs of eighteenth century British capitalism. In the early eighteenth century Ireland provided a market

1

for British manufactured goods and an inflow of capital to England in the form of rents and raw materials. At the same time the Crown prevented the development of a local industrial base by granting monopolies in industry and commerce to British investors in Ireland.

By the second half of the eighteenth century the low costs of labor associated with food production in Ireland resulted in the export of inexpensive foodstuffs for the British industrial classes. The availability of a relatively cheap food supply helped to control unrest among British workers and fueled the industrial revolution. Further, Irish primary products such as wool and flax were exchanged unequally for British goods. Until the middle of the eighteenth century, Ireland raised meat that was exported to plantations of the Caribbean. In 1689 a publication entitled The Interest of England in the Preservation of Ireland stated that "The islands and plantations of America are in a manner sustained by vast quantities of beef, pork, butter and other provisions of the product of Ireland" (O'Donovan, 1940:73). However, with the advent of industrialization in England, Ireland was put to work raising grain in order to provide cheap food for the English industrial classes. In addition, the American Revolution and the war with France deprived Britain of food resources which Ireland then supplied. O'Donovan (1940:114-116) notes that in the 1760s Ireland exported 213,000 barrels of beef of which 50% went to plantations in the American Colonies, 48% to Europe and 1% to England. By 1800 the island nation exported 147,382 barrels with 70% of the total shipped to England. Between 1771-73 Ireland exported 31,423 barrels of grain but by 1791 grain exports rose to 863,000 barrels while Irish beef exports fell by 1/3 (Newenham, 1805).

The effects of this system of exploitation on the socioeconomic status of Ireland were profound. Ireland developed two agricultural systems, a bare subsistence agriculture alongside a profitable commercial agriculture. Subsistence farmers who lived on a diet of potatoes, turnips and oats were put to work raising livestock, wheat, oats and barley for export. Within a single holding two zones existed, one for cash crops which usually utilized the best soils, and one for subsistence crops on the poorer land. However, as marginal acreage was improved, subsistence croplands were often converted to cash tillage in order to pay rising rents. Thus, landlord pressure for more rents led to subsistence crops being pushed on to the least desirable land. Tenants did not receive any equity benefits as a result of improving the land. In addition to the tenant farmers, a group of laborers known as cottiers exchanged their labor on the landlord's estate for dwarf holdings that would afford a bare subsistence.

Absentee landlords, most of them English, hired agents to manage their Irish farms and estates. The intermediaries, who were often Irish, exploited the peasants who rented or worked the lord's acreage. In some cases the agent imposed conditions reminiscent of medieval feudalism; in others, the middleman enriched himself by insisting upon a commission from each tenant. Across the land it was accepted policy to increase the following year's rent reflecting any improvements the peasant family had made to better their home or fields. As a result of those oppressive customs, the Irish peasant class found it almost impossible to raise their standard of living.

English landlords employing Irish-born agents found that the native men served as a buffer against criticism. If an Irishman exploited another Irishman, who could possibly blame the absentee landowner? So as Ireland's most avaricious sons exploited their own countrymen, the degraded peasantry slipped toward disaster. Poorer and poorer land was brought under cultivation for subsistence farming. Tenant farmers and cottiers grew potatoes for an entire family on fractional acreage while raising more cash crops on higher, drier land. As population increased, competition for fields led to higher rents, pushing the poorest peasants onto wastelands. There, they worked boggy, stony or terraced land in an ever more difficult struggle to pay rent, taxes and tithe. The system effectively blocked rural economic development in Ireland, but allowed agents to grow fat in the manor house, landlords to live in luxury, and Irish peasants to exist on the brink of disaster.

In the early nineteenth century, particularly in the years following the

Napoleonic Wars, many landlords cleared their estates, often through evictions. Thus began a slow but steady shift toward a more capital-intensive agriculture based on pasturage rather than tillage. This trend was more prevalent in the most fertile areas of Ireland, especially the east and southeast. Ireland, it seems, was to become a "cattle farm" for Britain. By forcing many Irish peasants off the land two things were accomplished. It created a home market for food among landless wage earners and helped to expand the so-called "industrial reserve army" of potential workers. This "army" served as a threat to British workers in the form of potential competition for jobs, as well as a source of low-paid immigrant additions to the British work force.

Peasants responded to the shift in tillage by delaying marriage and having fewer children. These demographic changes were an adaptive, grassroots response to socioeconomic changes and the waning economic value of children in the emerging economic situation. However, these trends started at least two decades before the Great Starvation, and were not a response to it as some writers have claimed.

The Act of Union in 1803, a scheme which was purportedly designed to combine the parliaments of Ireland and Great Britain into a single entity, was defeated when first introduced in the Dublin Parliament in 1799. Britain, determined to unite the two countries, resorted to bribery, freely distributing peerage and purse among the corrupt members of the Irish Legislature. In 1800 the bill was passed by a majority of sixty, although one hundred still opposed the measure. Thus a corrupt and nonrepresentative Irish Parliament (further coerced by 100,000 British soldiers occupying their land) abetted England in tightening her hold over her oft-rebellious colony. Henceforth Ireland's economy, previously quite prosperous, would be exploited, her industries would collapse, and her agricultural surplus would be exported to feed Britain's growing industrial proletariat.

The exploitation of Ireland's resources had increased substantially during the Napoleonic Wars. Irish agriculture helped sustain England in the years between 1803-05 when the French and their allies had nearly isolated Britain in the depths of the struggle. During the next decade rising exports of Irish grain and livestock fed both the English soldiers and the masses producing war materials in the factories.

Following Napoleon's defeat in 1815 a post-war depression rocked the British economy, creating problems for Irish farmers. Wheat prices fell by one third prompting the London Parliament to pass the Corn Law. This legislation, ostensibly enacted to "save the farmer" excluded imported grain (except from captive Ireland) from the British Isles until the price of domestic cereals reached a profitable target price in the marketplace. Although the law led to continued growth in the export of grain from Ireland to England, guaranteed minimum prices favored the landlords and led to greater dependence on the potato.

The Irish masses had few political rights and were entirely at the mercy of the landlord class and British colonial administrators. Arthur Young (1780), who traveled widely in Ireland, observed:

"A landlord in Ireland can scarcely invent an order which a laborer, servant, or cottier dares to refuse. He may punish with his cane or horsewhip with the most perfect security. A poor man would have his bones broken if he offered to lift a hand in his own defense."

The Potato and the Irish Peasant

The potato was domesticated by indigenous South American peoples at least six thousand years ago. These natives of the Central Andean Plateau devised a simple potato agriculture that produced sizeable yields with little investment in labor and few tools. Later, the crop became a staple food throughout the vast Inca empire. Following their conquest of the Inca, the Spanish introduced the potato into Europe in the mid-sixteenth century. By 1600 cultivation of the tuber had expanded into most areas of the continent.

In the first four decades of the seventeenth century the potato spread throughout Ireland. By 1700 it had replaced grain as a staple, becoming a more important foodstuff in Ireland than in any other European nation. The potato, ideally suited to the biocultural situation in Ireland, was quickly adopted by the Irish.

Adapting the crop to local conditions, the Irish planted their potatoes in "lazy beds." These plots, known as *iomairí*, in Ireland's Gaelic-speaking regions, required more labor than the term implies. Working in a family or communal effort, farmers laid seed potatoes on the ground in a straight line. Wherever the terrain permitted, the rows ran downhill to facilitate drainage. Finally, earth from trenches dug on either side of the potatoes was heaped over the tubers to a depth of eight to twelve inches. This methodology, which required only a hoe and a spade, allowed the Irish to achieve maximum productivity from the small plots situated on the edge of bogs, on terraced hillsides, and on the poor soils of Connacht.

Environmental conditions were excellent: the soil was deep, friable and acidic, while the climate was mild, characterized by heavy rains, brisk moist winds and high humidity during the growing seasons. The oceanic location of Ireland and the Gulf Stream modified the temperatures so that they ranged from 20 to 81 degrees Fahrenheit. There was also an absence of ecological enemies such as aphids.

The potato was a food that produced a large yield from a small acreage, while at the same time required minimal cultivation and labor and little money for seed. Its method of cultivation easily fit into the hoe and spade agriculture already existent in Ireland. Further, the system of land tenure, characterized by small holdings, was well suited to a crop that would maximize productivity. Harvests of over five tons of potatoes from a single acre of Ireland's black peat soils were not uncommon. Understandably, most landlords encouraged their tenants to grow the tuber, freeing more land for cash crops. According to Coote (1801:191-193) the potato was one of the few major crops not subject to tithe. Adam Smith in his classic, The Wealth of Nations, considered the potato to be an excellent food for the lower classes. After observing Irish immigrants in London he concluded that "it made men stronger and women more beautiful" (Smith, 1937:160-61).

The potato was a crop ideally suited to the turbulent sociopolitical conditions of seventeenth century Ireland, which included wars and rebellions. Potatoes were not easily trampled by cavalry and did not require warehouses that could be burned by marauding armies. From a domestic point of view the potato fit the customary Irish cooking practices which emphasized the boiling of food. Thus, potatoes did not require new utensils or more fuel. It was also easily stored over long periods of time, if kept in a cool, dark place. Finally, it was a nutritious, filling food source when combined with milk and butter.

The success of the potato allowed the population to increase while the size of the average landholding was decreasing. The Irish population steadily increased from the mid-eighteenth century on. For example, between 1779-1841 the population multiplied 172%, while during the same period the English population rose by 88%. Ireland's population expanded from two and one half million in 1700 to five and one quarter million by 1800. On the eve of the Great Starvation it had risen to well over eight million, and possibly approached ten million. The mass of the population was precariously dependent on the potato for survival, especially in the west and southwest. It is estimated that seven out of ten Irish families lived at subsistence level with little or no surplus money at the time of the famine (Lysaght, 1986).

The significance of the large number of pigs in pre-starvation Ireland has been ignored or de-emphasized by many modern scholars. Historians frequently quote passages which describe Irish tenant farmers and cottiers sharing the same humble cabin with the family's swine. This amply illustrates the extreme poverty of the peasants and helps create and maintain the illusion of Malthusian overcrowding. These well-chosen quotes, however, rarely contain any mention of the important role of swine in the economics of Ireland's rural households during the eighteenth and nineteenth centuries. An omnivorous feeder, the family pig was fattened at little cost. Its diet consisted primarily of potato wastes, supplemented by turnip trimmings and whatever other edibles it could forage in the dooryard. By virtue of their well-known habit of consuming garbage and rodent pups, pigs helped keep rats and mice in check. In addition, the pigs supplied a considerable quantity of manure, an essential ingredient in soil revitalization.

In most cases, the peasant family did not consume any of the pork that they raised. Mature pigs were destined for the market. Prior to the starvation, it may be assumed that the sale of an extra pig or two occasionally financed passage to America for a fortunate son or daughter. Such occurrences, however, were probably quite rare. Usually, the market value of the animals, combined with that of a few sacks of grain, provided just enough income to pay the rent. Anything left over was needed to pay the tithe to the Anglican Church. As Gallagher (1982:21) so aptly stated: "With England's help, the potato and the pig created and sustained the squalor . . .", for the majority of Irish-raised swine were shipped to Britain where they supplied bacon for the industrial workers and their families.

Another important commodity in the peasant economy was peat. More commonly known as turf, this was the primary fuel source for approximately one million rural Irish families on the eve of the Starvation. Each summer Irish men, women and children spent two or three weeks in the bogs cutting and stacking blocks of peat to dry in the wind. If they could not barter a portion of their harvest for cartage, Irish families spent an additional week transporting the year's fuel supply to their homes. In addition to providing an affordable medium for heating and cooking, the annual turf harvest helped reclaim boglands for potato fields.

During this discussion regarding the population of Ireland we feel it appropriate to correct a long-standing misconception, and to compare and contrast Ireland, an island colony, with other western European nations which also suffered loss of their potato crops. First, Disraeli's 1841 speech which claimed that Ireland was the most densely-populated country in Europe, is incorrect. Even if we place the Irish population in 1841 at nine million persons, we arrive at a density of 276.2 persons per square mile. Belgium, which had 4,073,162 inhabitants in 1840, was even more crowded with 308.24 persons/sq. mi. Saxony, a German kingdom in that era, was equally replete (DeBow 1853). Table I, on the following page, offers

Select European Populations on the Eve of the Starvation

Nation	Population	Year	Area (sq. mi.)	Density
Belgium	4,073,162	1840	13,215	308.22
England & Wales	14,997,427	1841	58,582	256.01
France & Corsica	34,213,427	1841	203,736	167.93
Denmark	1,227,384	1840	21,836	56.21
Netherlands	2,860,450	1840	13,589	210.50
Norway	1,328,471	1845	291,164	4.56
Ireland	**8,196,597**	**1841**	**32,589**	**251.51**
Scotland	2,620,184	1841	30,414	86.15
Bavaria*	4,370,581	1843	29,637	147.47
Hanover*	1,761,632	1843	14,734	119.56
Wirtemberg*	1,752,538	1846	7,640	229.39
Saxony*	1,757,800	1843	5,750	305.7
Baden*	1,296,967	1840	5,904	219.68
Hesse-Cassel*	754,702	1846	4,430	170.36

Source: DeBow 1853 : xxxiv
* Select German States (Germany did not coalesce into a unified nation until the 1870s).

16

an overview of select European populations prior to the great starvation.

Irish population growth is often blamed sigularly on the availablitity and productivity of the potato. But population growth in Ireland, as in less developed countries today, was related to the expansion of opportunities in labor markets. In Ireland's situation the expansion of raising grain and grain-fed beef for English markets, and the rise of the flax and linen yarn production as a cottage industry, increased the demand for rural laborers. This scenario obviously called for larger families.

The adoption of the potato was an adaptive response to economic circumstances. As Irish exports of grain, livestock and flax increased, the proportion of quality farmland devoted to these products expanded accordingly. This shift forced native farmers onto marginal croplands and onto wastelands. Consequently, the potato, the only high-yielding crop that would prosper on these soils, became the staple foodstuff for Ireland's peasants. Another Irish peasant adaptation to marginality was the development of co-operative work groups that were used to work poor land, as well as harvest the peat necessary for heat and cooking. It should be noted, however, that Irish population growth started in 1750, a date long after the potato was introduced.

Between 1775 and 1815 there was a boom in Irish agriculture resulting from the collapse of European agriculture during a turbulent period which included the French Revolution and the Napoleonic Wars. During this era, Irish agricultural products filled the gap in production. Although a portion of Ireland's increased output was a result of technological advances, the prime characteristic of Irish agriculture in that era was human power. Most native farmers were unable to afford recently-developed implements, planting and harvesting the improved varieties with dated tools and massed labor. Much of the Irish population increase during this period was among the cottier class. The cottiers were landless peasants who contracted with a landlord to work for him in exchange for a potato patch and a cabin. The cottier increase during this period was a response to expansion of tillage agriculture which was so labor-intensive.

Ross (1985) has proposed that the spread of spinning linen yarn in the late eighteenth and early nineteenth centuries had an important impact on Irish population growth. Spinning, a good source of farm income, required considerable labor to harvest and prepare the fiber. Flax must be pulled up by the root, retted (a fermentation process) and the fibers stripped from the woody core of the stalk. On Irish and Scotch farms women and children provided the extra hands necessary to perform these tasks. Thus, all family members contributed to the household economy. The English encouraged this Irish cottage industry because the newly-developed British power loom industry desperately needed linen yarn to provide a strong warp for cotton cloth.

Flax raising was quite suitable for small farms and it was in western Connacht, an area of very poor small farms that the industry developed most heavily. The fibrous plant grew well after potatoes, and crop rotation soon developed. Flax yielded a larger return per unit cropped than most other commercial crops. It was also exempt from tithe tax, and certainly production of

Factors in the Success of the Potato in Ireland

Biophysical	Sociocultural
Biological	**Social**
1. Absence of ecological enemies, such as aphids;	1. System of land tenure encouraged it, e.g. small subsistence plots;
2. High yield on a small parcel of land withoug a large capital investment.	2. Ideally suited for the turbulent sociopolitical conditions of the 17th century, e.g. wars, rebellion (couldn't be trampled and no warehouses to destroy);
Geophysical	3. Required little capital and allowed time to work on cash crops to pay rent.
1. The climate and soil were right;	**Technological**
2. Heavy rain, brisk moist winds, with high humidity during the growing season;	1. Method of cultivation easily fitted the implements already in use, e.g. hoe, spade;
3. Deep friable acid soils.	2. Fitted the customary methods (no new utensils, fuel efficient, easy to store).
4. Ocean modified temperature (20° to 81°F).	

linen yarn added much-needed income to the small family farm.

According to Ross these developments led to a number of demographic changes: an increased rate of marriage, a trend toward younger marriage, and increased fecundity. It is interesting to note that records indicate that Irish population growth peaked at about the time when linen export had tripled. However, Irish fertility was not only spurred by the value of children as workers. Traditionally the Irish held children, and having children, in great esteem, and as in less developed areas today, children were a sort of old age insurance.

After examining these facts, it becomes clear that the dependence of the Irish on the potato was the adaptive choice of the Irish peasant. It was the result of the social, political and economic conditions under which they were forced to live. The colonial system in Ireland allowed rents so high that only barest portions of the land could be used for subsistence. Landlordism promoted the potato, as a dietary staple, and Irish peasants, locked into a colonial system that denied them control of their native soil, were forced to adopt the tuber as a means of basic survival.

Illustrated London News

Funeral at Shepperton Lakes

Ireland on the Eve of the Great Starvation

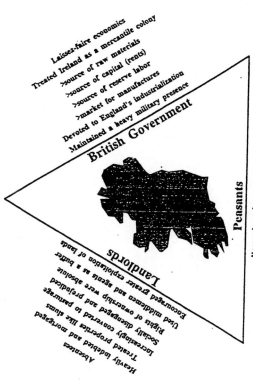

British Government

Laissez-faire economics
Treated Ireland as a mercantile colony
>source of raw materials
>source of capital (rents)
>source of reserve labor
>market for manufactures
Devoted to England's industrialization
Maintained a heavy military presence

Peasants

Heavy dependence on the potato
Producers of food for export
Renting smaller and smaller holdings
Outside cash economy
Few rights and limited power
Dense population; but not over-populated

Landlords

Absentee
Heavily indebted and mortgaged
Treated properties like slums
Increasingly disengaged and prejudiced
Rights of ownership and agents were absolute
Used middlemen and agents as a buffer
Encouraged greater exploitation of lands
Socially converted to pastures

Illustrated London News

Family Viewing Rotting Potatoes

II
Ireland on the Eve of Starvation

Prior to 1845, pre-starvation Ireland was characterized by primitive technology, a colonial social organization dictated by an exploitive political policy, and an economic system that did not reinvest in Ireland. Agricultural technology was narrow and undeveloped while no significant industry existed except in northeast Ulster. Commerce lagged by the European standards of the day and medical technology was grossly deficient, even in the most rudimentary form. At the onset of the starvation there were only 39 infirmaries for care of the ill in all of Ireland. In the County Mayo, this element of imperial neglect resulted in a ratio of one infirmary per 366,000 people.

The social organization of Ireland was characterized by a ruling landlord class often represented by a small class of agents, and

Illustrated London News

**Boy and Girl Searching
for Potatoes in Caheragh**

26

a mass of powerless peasants of varying social status. The land owners were often absentees, heavily in debt and mortgaged to the limit in order to maintain their upper-class lifestyle. Kennedy estimated that absentee rents between 1810 and 1842 ranged from £2 to £6 million a year (1973:34). Their Irish properties were treated much like modern slum properties, with high rents, more than 80% higher than those in England, and no improvements. In areas where there was less land available for subsistence the limited number of available plots led to competition among the Irish peasants, so the rents were raised further. In Galway, on the Dillon estate, rents increased 51% between 1767 and 1780. Furthermore, the landlords were socially separated from the masses and were looked upon as an alien nationality. The agents or middlemen, who often managed the properties, encouraged exploitation and neglect of the tenants, including extortion and eviction, in order to increase their own profits. Add to this the fact that landlords maintained an ideology of racial superiority toward the natives, and, thus, had poor perceptions of the Irish as human beings.

Landlords were responsible for maintaining workhouses in their districts and were assessed a poor tax to meet those obligations. In order to avoid paying high poor tax rates tenants were often evicted so the landlord could claim that people crowding into the workhouse were not from his district. Unlike their English counterparts, evicted Irish peasants had no legal recourse. The right of private property was absolute in Ireland. This alone indicates that the Act of Union was a sham.

Although everyone worked in the planting and harvest seasons, chronic unemployment was characteristic of rural Ireland during most of the year. According to an 1837 British government report, 2,385,000 Irish were out of work for at least thirty weeks out of the year (Woodham-Smith, 1962:32). Even in the best of times Irish peasants had no hope of finding other work as general labor for there were few internal improvements and public works projects. Most of them lived outside of the cash economy so they could not purchase food even if it were available at cheap prices. The Irish peasant had been reduced to the status of a producer of cheap food for export, with few political rights and no power.

Irish peasants rented smaller and smaller holdings as rents became more oppressive and less land was available. By 1841 45% of the holdings were less than 5 acres, and several hundred thousand parcels were under 1 acre (Rubenstein, 1983:100). Early marriage became the rule because there was little chance of accumulating wealth, so delay offered no reward. The landlords also encouraged early marriage in order to create more domestic units which could pay more rent in grain. It was possible to maintain a minimal subsistence because of the potato's productivity and the availability of relatively cheap shelter and fuel. A single acre of potatoes could provide for a family of six along with a pig and some chickens. The average Irish peasant consumed daily 10 to 14 pounds of potatoes per adult and about 5 pounds per child. From a nutritional standpoint, potatoes provided a relatively well-balanced diet. The only deficiency, vitamin A, was remedied by the seasonal availability of whole milk. A cabin or cottage was easily and cheaply built in less than a day, while furniture and clothing were very basic. One couldn't be poorer and certainly the chances were very slim that you would get richer, so why postpone marriage? It is estimated that on the eve of the starvation, 7 out of 10 families lived at the subsistence level with little or no extra cash.

Until 1838 Irish peasants were also obliged to pay taxes to the Anglican Church that they did not attend (McDowell, 1957). Agrarian violence, focused in part on the tithe issue, rose in the 1830s. All Irish, regardless of their religious beliefs, were required to contribute one tenth of their income to the upkeep of the Anglican Church. Foster (1988) attributes a portion of the increase in the activities of secret societies to over-reaction by police and clergy. The "Tithe War", combined with political pressure from O'Connell's repeal movement, brought about the passage of the Commutation Act of 1838. The Act, however, simply transferred the assessment to the land owner. In turn, the owners raised rents to cover their increased costs, so that the peasants continued to shoulder the burden of support for the Anglican Church.

At this time, the British government was interested in the industrialization of Britain,

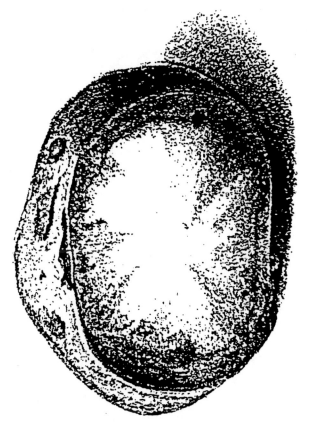

potato blight (phytophora infestans)

U.S. Department of Agriculture, 1888.

Cross Section of a Blighted Potato

not Ireland. It adhered to a laissez-faire theory of political economy. Ireland was treated as a mercantilist colony; a source of raw materials, capital, labor reserves, a market for manufactured goods and a producer of cheap food for the British industrial classes. Inexpensive foodstuffs were necessary in order to suppress English wages, holding them to a point equal to competition abroad, and to prevent working class dissent and protest that would threaten economic and social stability. Ireland also served as a source of soldiers for British colonial armies. In fact, many Irish could eat Irish meat only when they joined the British army. In short, Ireland was governed in the interests of British capitalism and imperialism.

III
The Progress of the Starvation

The Potato Failure and Starvation

The potato blight (phytophora infestans) was introduced from America by way of Europe in 1845. It appeared first in Wexford and Waterford in September, after a long wet summer. It spread rapidly until over half the country was affected. By July and August of the following year, 1846, potato crop failure was complete throughout Ireland. It was followed by an unusually harsh winter. The westerly winds failed and cold from Scandinavia and Russia moved into the island.

Weakened by starvation and ravaged by the severe cold, the Irish population was ripe for the spread of disease. Respiratory disease became widespread and contributed to high mortality among starved and weakened peasants. In 1847, typhus epidemics spread among the refugees from the countryside adding to the rising mortality as the displaced peasants crowded into urban areas in search of food. Cholera, dysentery, typhus and relapsing fever decimated local populations. For example, Whelan (1994:28) found in a sample of 4,000 dead from west Cork in 1847 that 44% died of fever, 34% of starvation and 22% from dysentery. Scurvy, due to vitamin C deficiency, contributed to mortality rates, while vitamin A deficiency led to eye problems including blindness, as well as higher mortality rates, especially in children. Between early 1846 and the end of 1848, two million of Ireland's 8,500,000 citizens were lost to starvation or emigration. Conservative estimates suggest that at least one million persons died of starvation or related disease in the first five years of the disaster. Some scholars, however, have found evidence that the total number of deaths for the seven-year period (1846-52) is most likely nearer 1,500,000 and possibly as high as two million.

According to Don Mullan 200 to 300 mass graves, each containing over one thousand bodies have been identified (Campbell, 1994:23). An island off the coast of Donegal has been known as the "Island of the Dead" since it was used for a mass grave during the starvation. Inside the ruins of a Cistercian abbey at Abbeystrewery, County Cork, more than nine thousand people are buried in a mass grave. Some records from County Clare indicate that between 1846 and 1847 45,000 died in Clare alone. The deaths of children, a dependant class, were often not recorded. In many areas the infant mortality rate reached 50%, especially in the winter of 1847. In fact, so many of the local deaths from starvation were never recorded that we will never know the true extent of its quantitative impact. As Patrick Campbell notes:

> Out in the hills and bogs beyond Dungloe, those who died were often buried in the bog without ceremony, or were burned at the bottom of the garden with other family members who had died, with no wake and no funeral. Death had become so common by 1848 it seemed to make no sense to fuss about it, and the disposal of bodies was prompt

and without fanfare--and life went
on for the survivors (1995).

The onset of the starvation was a
biometeorological phenomenon; the British
reaction to the situation was sociopolitical.
Government relief was reluctant, meager and
irrelevant to true solutions. The London
Parliament would not alter established
economic policies to accommodate the
disaster. No free food could be distributed
while private dealers offered similar
commodities for sale. Charitable groups
were not permitted to undersell merchants.
Aid shipments from other nations were also
withheld from the starving Irish. One
particularly blatant example involved a
warship full of grain donated by the people
of Massachusetts. The ship was allowed to
land its cargo but the food was put in
storage for distribution at a later date.
Other Americans, moved by the
disaster, also contributed substantial
amounts of aid to Ireland's starving millions.
The citizens of New York also sent a
shipload of relief supplies in 1847, and
dozens of cities and towns organized
collections of money, food and clothing for

shipment to Ireland. One such outpouring of generosity came from the Choctaw Nation which had been exiled to wastelands west of the Mississippi during the 1830s. Despite their own marginal status the Choctaws contributed an impressive sum toward Irish relief.

British claims of transportation difficulties encountered in shipping and distributing relief supplies in Ireland are false. Between 1845 and 1850 the number of merchant ships registered in the United Kingdom rose from 24,388 to 25,984, an increase of 1,596 vessels. The additional 1,375,000 tons could have shipped sufficient relief supplies to Ireland entirely in British hulls (Mitchell, 1992:693). Internal distribution of imported foodstuffs would have been possible using Ireland's existing transportation network.

Oliver McDonagh (1976:396-7) states that at the onset of the famine nearly every Irish citizen lived within ten miles of a major road, canal or railroad. Foreign grain and other relief supplies could have been shipped on these routes just as efficiently as Irish produce had traditionally been transported to seaports for export to

England. There were more than half a million horses in Ireland during the 1840s, but a fair proportion of the livestock employed in transporting Irish agricultural products during the famine were engaged in hauling Irish grain, paid as rents, for export. In September of 1846 Sir Randolph Routh estimated the value of oats alone being exported from Ireland to pay rent at £60,000.

"It must be remembered that there was still enough wheat, oats, barley, butter, eggs, beef, pork and lamb in Ireland, even in this famine year of 1847, to feed for a year four times as many people as were leaving the country. But all this produce was still being sent to Liverpool on the very same ships that carried the emigrants, whom the English lawmakers claimed could not be fed, were redundant in their native land, and therefore had to go somewhere else." (Gallagher, 1982:148-9) ... " On one ship alone, the steamer Ajax, which sailed from Cork in 1847 for

England, the cargo consisted of 1,514 firkins[*] of butter, 102 casks of pork, 44 hogsheads of whiskey, 844 sacks of oats, 247 sacks of wheat, 106 bales of bacon, 13 casks of hams, 145 casks of porter, 12 sacks of fodder, 28 bales of feathers, 8 sacks of lard, 296 boxes of eggs, 30 head of cattle, 90 pigs, 220 lambs, 34 calves and 69 miscellaneous packages." (The Nation, October 16, 1847 in Gallagher, 1982:148-9)

---

[*]Firkin = British unit of measure equal to one fourth of a barrel.

Genesis of the Great Starvation

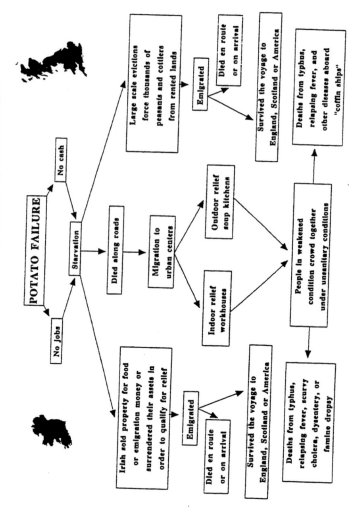

POTATO FAILURE

No jobs

No cash

Starvation

Died along roads

Large scale evictions force thousands of peasants and cottiers from rented lands

Emigrated

Died en route or on arrival

Survived the voyage to England, Scotland or America

Deaths from typhus, relapsing fever, and other diseases aboard "coffin ships"

Migration to urban centers

Outdoor relief soup kitchens

Indoor relief workhouses

People in weakened condition crowd together under unsanitary conditions

Irish sold property for food or emigration money or surrendered their assets in order to qualify for relief

Emigrated

Died en route or on arrival

Survived the voyage to England, Scotland or America

Deaths from typhus, relapsing fever, scurvy cholera, dysentery, or famine dropsy

Illustrated London News

The USS Macedonian , filled with Irish relief supplies donated by the people of Massachusetts

The British policy of non-intervention in the crisis was at best uneven throughout the British Isles. The potato crop had failed throughout most of Europe in 1846, threatening widespread disaster. Other governments distributed free food to peasants. Louis Philippe ordered France's military warehouses to dole out their foodstuffs to the starving millions in that country. Belgium, Holland and the German States also took extensive measures in an effort to avert starvation. Britain on the other hand, continued to adhere to laissez-faire policy as far as Ireland was concerned, while preventing outright starvation in the rest of the kingdom.

The Highlands of Scotland had experienced a similar pattern of population growth, dependence on the potato, and subdivisions of marginal agricultural lands, creating an impoverished class of crofters similar to Ireland's cottiers. When the full force of the potato blight struck the area in 1846, the potential for starvation among Scottish tenant farmers was equal to that of Irish peasants and cottiers. But the government and landlords of Scotland devised ways to circumvent official non-intervention policies and prevent widespread loss of life. Although there were isolated instances where Scottish peasants starved to death as a result of crop failure and evictions, most of Scotland was spared the tragedy that befell Ireland.

England also endured shortages during the famine years. While Ireland experienced an unusually wet summer in 1845, England received an even greater amount of precipitation, with heavy rains destroying a portion of the harvest. Thus, when the potato blight struck the United Kingdom in full force the following year, England had little in the way of food reserves to meet the disaster, neither at home nor in Ireland or Scotland. Ireland began to starve while England tripled its imports of wheat, barley, oats and flour between 1845 and 1847. Maize imports into the United Kingdom rose from £24 million in 1845 to £1,546 million sterling in 1847.

Most historians have implied that English relief efforts attempted to feed Ireland's starving millions, but Irish cereal production, combined with UK imports of maize in 1847, would have supplied an Irish population of 9,000,000 with an average of

Illustrated London News

An Irish Village During the Starvation

more than 700 pounds of grain per person. Taking the demographic factors of the Irish population into consideration (the high percentage of young children who consume far less than a 150 pound adult) and assuming that dairy production remained constant (the number of cattle in Ireland rose from 1,863,000 in 1841 to 2,967,000 in 1851) it appears that Ireland would have suffered no more than France or Belgium during the potato failures of the late 1840s. But large quantities of Irish oats, wheat and barley were exported to England to pay rents, leaving Ireland critically short of foodstuffs. Such grain as England shipped to Ireland was usually maize, nutritionally inferior to wheat, oats or barley and outside of the traditional Irish peasant diet. England's imports, however, just barely managed to feed the destitute millions in her own agricultural districts and the crofters in the Scottish Highlands.

It is possible that the government failed to grasp the magnitude of the failure and its potential human impact. However, this is difficult to believe given the efficiency of Britain's military machine in Ireland with its very massive, effective intelligence systems.

Relief was inadequate both in absolute and relative terms. Most of the British contribution was in the form of loans that had to be repaid. For example, between 1846 and 1849, £15,000,000 was spent on direct relief and food, which was probably a little more than .03% of the British GNP. In 1833, however, the London Government spent £20,000,000 to buy out slave owners in the West Indies and Africa (Gibbon, 1975). It is interesting to note in this context that in 1666, after the Great Fire of London the Irish provided 20,000 cattle to London for relief. Mokyr notes that less than a decade later, in the mid-1850s, Britain was willing to spend £69.3 million on the Crimean War. In the 1860s the Lancashire "cotton famine" moved the British to relax the poor laws and to grant a subsidized loan of £1.5 million for public works (O'Grada, 1988).

The legal system abetted the landlords rather than aiding the stricken peasantry. It allowed landlords to apply to the courts for judgment against tenants who were in arrears. As soon as a delinquency proceeding was filed the tenants took their belongings and fled because the judgment could result in a prison sentence. A prison sentence would leave one's family to fend for themselves, a virtual death sentence at that time in Ireland. This tactic helped to clear the land of people, without eviction, and released the landlords from Poor Tax obligations. As the Starvation progressed, the London Parliament passed additional legislation aiding the landlords intent on eviction.

The Encumbered Estates Acts of 1848 and 1849 were ostensibly introduced in an effort to facilitate speedy sales of near-bankrupt properties by their owners. In theory, wealthy English capitalists would purchase neglected estates from spendthrift landlords, improve the properties and thereby reverse the declining value of Irish agricultural land. In reality, the Encumbered Estates Acts hastened the eviction rate. The Act of 1849 allowed owners and creditors to appeal to the courts for quick liquidation of their estates. Manors and farms were then sold, sweeping away all tenants' rights and opening the way for further clearance of land. This action also reduced the landlord's poorhouse assessment.

In 1846, Prime Minister Robert Peel finally decided to repeal the Corn Laws, some say, in order to help the situation in Ireland. Others suggest that he simply used the situation in Ireland as a pretext to eliminate protective measures with which he disagreed. Foreign grain was supposed to inundate England and drive the price of food down. This did not happen and grain continued to be exported from Ireland while the failure was in progress. It is estimated that enough grain was exported to feed the population of the whole island (Woodham-Smith, 1962). Even cheap grain would not have helped, since more grain would have been needed to pay rents, thus dropping more farmers below the failure level. It was the speculators who benefitted most from the repeal. Irish grain bought in England was shipped to Ireland to be sold at half price as a relief effort, but peasants did not have money to buy it. So, speculators bought it and resold it in England to relief agencies and the cycle started over again. Some grain shipments were apparently sold several times in this manner. The people needed free food, not price deflation.

Henry Drummond, a member of Parliament, chaired a committee in Dublin,

which suggested the following immediate measures:
1. Stop export of grain and distilling of grain into spirits.
2. Remove duties on food imports.
3. Public works that would concentrate on railroad and harbor infrastructures as well as drainage projects.
4. Relief committees should be funded in part by a 10% tax on landlords (20 - 50% on absentees).
5. And in part by a £1.5 million sterling/10 year loan from Britain with Irish hardwood forests as security.

However, Peel ignored all its recommendations, except #2, as he repealed the Corn Law.

A public works program was carried out between 1846 and 1848. People were paid to build useless roads to nowhere and functionless walls in the countryside, under conditions similar to Nazi Germany. Many people were too weak to do such physically demanding work, but over 3,000,000 Irish became dependent on it. The program was abolished in 1846, then briefly restored, then terminated in 1848, because it was too expensive.

It is interesting to note that little public money was spent to develop fisheries, harbors and railroads which would have had long-term benefits for the people and the economy. Fishing was never developed as a major industry in Ireland, mostly because the British resisted anything that might damage the Scottish fishing industry. As a result Ireland lacked a significant number of ships suitable for fishing and had insufficient means of transporting any substantial maritime harvest. In addition, the extreme poverty of most Irish fishermen precluded local investment. Some were too poor to afford salt to preserve their catch. In any case, the majority of Irish citizens lacked the money to buy fish, limiting the size of the domestic market. Finally, the difficult coastline and frequent fog contributed to the diminished importance of commercial fishing.

In 1847, Irish Board of Public Works Circular #8 proposed emergency legislation that would pay farm families to work their own land, and to work on drainage projects, but it was rejected by the British. John Stuart Mill, a member of parliament, suggested that the government buy wasteland and turn it over to the peasants for cultivation, but his proposal saw no action (O'Neill 1957). In 1845 the Devon Commission noted that waste land could be recovered making available 2.5 million acres of pasture land and 1.5 million acres for tillage. However, since there was no profit in it for the landlords, this land would not be made available to the Irish.

A Poor Law Amendment, known as the Gregory Clause, was enacted in 1847. It charged that no Irish peasant with at least a quarter of an acre of land was eligible for relief. This law forced tens of thousands to give up their land in order to get even minimal help. The people, thus dispossessed, headed in turn to the already crowded urban areas, soup kitchens and workhouses. A few landlords paid shipfares to help their tenants emigrate. They realized that the cost of shipping their impoverished peasants off to Canada was less than the expense incurred keeping the paupers in the workhouse for a year. Further, it was a cost only incurred once. Landlords most frequently subsidized the most dependent of their Irish tenants, the old and the sick. Even so these landlords were scarce, and most money for emigration came from friends and relatives in America. Emigration, however, often only presented the emigrant with a 50% chance of survival. During the starvation years an estimated 15,000 to 20,000 recently-arrived Irish immigrants to Canada died and were buried on Grosse Ile, downstream from Quebec. These graves remain as a lasting testament to the perils of the trans-Atlantic voyage (Quigley, 1994:54). Many thousands more died enroute to or shortly after arrival at United States ports.

Beginning in March 1847 soup kitchens along with the workhouses, became the sole sources of aid to most victims. These kitchens were funded by private and church charities. The Quakers were particularly active in the endeavor. Some Protestant sects forced the natives to denounce Catholicism or the Virgin Mary before they were fed. Thus, underscoring the notion that even religious beliefs were fair game for the discriminatory actions taken at this time. Natives who collaborated in· this way were referred to locally as "soupers." The menu at the kitchens consisted of weak soup and bread; hardly enough to keep one alive. It is estimated that there was one soup kitchen for every 20,000 people. Margaret Crawford (1989) suggests that the watery soups were not what starving people needed. Starving people are often suffering from water retention due to nutritional edema. Additional fluid intake further complicates such a condition and most likely leads to increased mortality. O'Grada has also suggested that authorities may have thought soup would minimize cheating since it was not easy to transport or sell (O'Grada, 1994:197).

Workhouses were overcrowded and unhealthy. According to Luke Dodd, curator of The Famine Museum at Strokestown, one could stand anywhere in Ireland and never be more then twenty miles from a workhouse. At the peak of the famine there were 173 workhouses operating in Ireland (Muligan, 1995). The Galway Vindicator noted that during "Black '49" the Limerick Workhouse, built for 800, housed 2,513 persons.

According to Cousens' (1960) excess mortality, except in Ulster, followed an west

Population Change 1841-1851

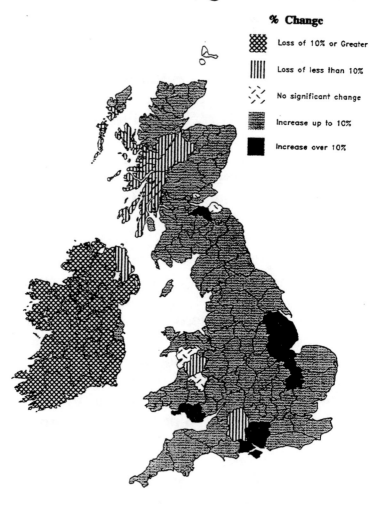

% Change

Loss of 10% or Greater

Loss of less than 10%

No significant change

Increase up to 10%

Increase over 10%

54

to east pattern from a high of 15 to 17.4 percent in Galway and Clare to a low of 2.5 to 7.4 percent along the east coast. Cousens makes the point that the impact of the starvation was regionally varied and that excess mortality varied from year to year. Joel Mokyr, professor of economics and history at Northwestern University, has recently shown that Cousen's estimates are probably lower in aggregate, and tend to overestimate in the east of Ireland and underestimate in the west. No county in Ireland, however, was left untouched by excessive death and suffering. The lowest rates were in Dublin and East Ulster.

Peasants tried to keep their produce, but troops and police were used to collect the food. Soldiers were assigned to guard depots, ships and harvest fields. In September, 1846, after food riots, a mobile force of 2000 troops was formed to quell food-related riots. In April, 1846 an official in Waterford said,

> "The barges leave Clonmel once a week for this place with the export supplies under convoy which, last Tuesday consisted of

2 guns, 50 cavalry, and 80 infantry escorting them on the banks of Suir as far as Carrick."

A prayer common in this time period, pleaded "We wish to God the government would send us food instead of soldiers" (McVeigh, nd).

O'Grada notes that peasant resistance, which was unorganized and sporadic, was ruthlessly suppressed. This may be gauged from the fact that hangings rose from six in 1843-46, to seventeen in 1848-49, while transportations for seven years rose from 485 to 1853 during the same era (O'Grada, 1994:204).

Eyewitness accounts document the destitution of the Irish masses as in an account from Mayo in 1849: "The streets are daily thronged with moving skeletons. The fields are strewn with dead ... the curse of Russell, more terrible than the curse of Cromwell is upon us...." William Forster, a Quaker Minister, commented on the children,

"...like skeletons, their features sharpened with hunger and their limbs wasted, so that there was little left but bones, their hands and arms in particular being much emaciated and the happy expressions of infancy gone from their faces, leaving the anxious look of premature old age...."

In 1846 Dr. Dominic Corrigan an Irish physician wrote in a pamphlet,

"Starve in the midst of plenty, as literally as if dungeon bars separated them from a granary. When distress has been at its height and our poor have been dying of starvation in our streets, our corn has been going to a foreign market. It is to our own poor, a forbidden fruit," (Corrigan, 1846).

In County Clare Lord Monteagel observed:

"People were eating food from which so putrid and offensive an effulvia issued that in consuming it they were obliged to leave the doors and windows of their cabins open," (Woodham-Smith, 1962).

However, in 1846 Colonel Henry Routh of the Relief Committee expressed the economic priorities of the British when he stated: "Even if it were practicable at the moment to open our depots it would be prejudicial to owners of grain in as much as at present extraordinary prices can be realized."
On March 13, 1846 the eviction of 300 tenants at Ballinglass was described:

> "The scene was frightful women running wailing with pieces of the property and clinging to door posts from which they had to be forcibly torn, men cursing, children screaming with fright. That night the people slept in the ruins. Next day they were driven out, the foundations of the houses torn up and razed and no neighbor was allowed to take them in (Woodham-Smith, 1962:71-72).

John Costello, a tenant of Invern near Galway, described a New Year's Eve eviction in 1847 as follows:

"He threw my three children out on the street; one of them was sick at the time; her name was Anne; she died last week; was near four years old; Coleman my son died on Friday last, aged ten years, from cold and hardship. My house was completely destroyed, and it was near dusk when it was thrown down; myself and my family had to sleep in the open air; it was raining and snowing that night, and it blew very hard; my wife and remaining child are now lying sick . . . in a hovel I made against the ruins of the house; when my child Coleman died there was over six inches of water about him." (Parliamentary Papers, 1847-48)

The <u>Limerick and Clare Examiner</u> in May 1848 noted:

"Nothing absolutely nothing is done to save the lives of the people -- they are swept out of their holdings without an effort on the part of our rulers to stay the violent progress of human destruction."

Any attempt to adequately describe the starvation is probably doomed from the start. Malcolm Brown (1972:94-95) in his book <u>Politics of Irish Literature</u> writes:

"The enormity of the famine has always been difficult to communicate. In struggling to illuminate the 'mere data' eyewitnesses found themselves baffled by the inadequacies of ordinary language. Indescribable, unbelievable, language would fail to give an adequate idea. Carlton himself protested , that his own words

60

were powerless to describe the famine terror."

In "The Famine Year" 1847 a poem by Jane Wilde (Speranza), we find the following:

"Our whitening bones against ye
    will rise as witness
From the cabins and the ditches,
    in their charred uncoffened
    masses.---
A ghastly spectral army, before
    the great God we'll stand
And arraign as our murderers the
    spoilers of our land."

An Irish American living in Ohio said that all that he had left of his famine ancestors was a note written by his great grandfather in an old Irish history book given to him by his uncle. The note reads: "Evicted by the English and abandoned by God."

Chronology of Starvation

September 1845	Potato blight appears in Wexford and Waterford and spread until half of Ireland was affected.
November 1845	Distribution of 100,000 pounds worth of Indian corn (maize) to destitute peasants.
February 1846	Food exports from Ireland's 1845 crop reach 1,000,000 pounds Sterling.
July/August 1846	Blight destroys the entire potato crop.
September 1846	Irish peasants killed and wounded when British troops fire upon unemployed Irishmen attempting to prevent export of grain from Port of Dungarvan.

Winter 1846-47	Unusually harsh weather combined with starvation and disease such as typhus and respiratory illness killing many thousands of Irish. Beginning of "Black '47".
January 1847	Soup Kitchen Act becomes law continuing the policy of charging Ireland with the costs of its own relief.
Summer 1847	Starvation continues and outbreaks of typhus, relapsing fever and dysentery sweep through the starving Irish.
Summer 1847	Exhausted Quakers shut down most relief operations in Ireland but continue long-term efforts to improve Ireland's plight through the distribution of seed.

July/August 1847	Few seed potatoes available. Small potato harvest gives some hope until landlords begin seizing grain harvest in lieu of rent.
Winter 1847-48	Parliament sends 15,000 more troops to Ireland to protect capital interests from starving peasantry.
Summer 1848	Complete failure of the potato crop; Young Irelanders' attempt an insurrection.
Autumn 1848	British Relief Association suspends activity in Ireland due to a shortage of funds. Poor Law remains only major entity administering relief in Ireland--at local expense.
1848 & 1849	English Parliament passes the Encumbered Estates Acts providing legal maneuver abetting rapid eviction of tenants.

December 1848	Outbreak of cholera begins its seven-month swath through Ireland, killing thousands weakened by hunger and deprivation.
August 1849	Limited potato harvest eases the situation somewhat but over 1,000,000 Irish have already died and similar numbers have emigrated.
Winter 1849-50	Deaths continue as the destitute who have neither the funds for food or shipfare suffer through another winter.
Spring 1850 - Spring 1851	The starvation begins to wind down, but more than half of Ireland is still at high risk.
Between 1848-1852	The starvation ran its course -- killing 1.5 to 2 million and forcing 1 to 1.5 million to emigrate.

Illustrated London News

A Village in County Clare During the Starvation

IV
The British Response

Hostility, prejudice and racism toward the Irish influenced the British approach to the Irish Famine. An attitude of absolute English supremacy in all things remained constant since the initial Norman Invasion of Ireland in the twelveth century (Lebow, 1977). Prominent clergymen blamed the Irish for reckless, improvident breeding and lack of morals. In 1847 Reverend Hugh McNeile of Liverpool, future Anglican Dean of Ripon, published a book, <u>The Famine a Rod of God: Its Provoking Cause, Its Merciful Design</u>, which echoed the theme of divine visitation. In 1848 the Anglican Archbishop of Dublin, Richard Whately, accused the Irish poor of responsibility for the circumstances in which they were placed, pointing to their slovenliness, inattention to religious duty and proneness to crime (O'Grada 1994:193). The <u>London Times</u> called for extermination, while <u>The Economist</u> referred to the Irish as primitive, incompetent, priest-ridden members of an inferior race. On February 12, 1853, <u>The Economist</u> wrote, "The departure of the redundant part of the population of Ireland and Scotland is an indispensable preliminary to every kind of improvement."

Punch, the British political humor magazine, depicted the Irish as the missing link between gorillas and negroes.

"A creature manifestly between the gorilla and the negro is to be met with in some of the lowest districts of London and Liverpool ...It belongs in fact to a tribe of Irish savages... When conversing with its kind it talks a sort of gibberish. It is, moreover, a climbing animal, and may sometimes be seen ascending a ladder laden with a hod of bricks."

The Irish were depicted as subhuman, so it was easier to excuse one's humanitarian obligations. In 1841 the English historian, J.A. Froude, described the Irish as being "more like tribes of squalid apes than human beings" (Kinealy, 1995:331). British intellectual views of the Irish were such that the British public widely hailed the starvation as an efficient solution to the "Irish problem." The Irish poor were lazy, morally depraved as well as subhuman, therefore they were undeserving of help. Dr. James Kay once wrote in a pamphlet:

> "But the most horrible spot lies on the Manchester side, immediately south-west of Oxford Road and is known as Little Ireland ...A hoard of ragged women and children swarm about here, as filthy as the swine that thrive upon the garbage heaps and in the puddles. In short, the whole rookery furnishes such a hateful and repulsive spectacle as can hardly be equalled in the worst court on the Irk. The race that lives in these ruinous cottages, behind broken windows, mended with oilskin, sprung doors, and rotten door-posts, or in dark, wet

69

cellars, in measureless filth and stench, in this atmosphere penned in as if with a purpose, this race must really have reached the lowest stage of humanity." (Kinealy 1995:330)

Misled by such tripe, many English were led to believe that the Irish were the cause of their own poverty and starvation. In other words, the English had turned effect into cause. If the perpetrator can place the blame on the victim, it allows one to live comfortably with the inhumanity of one's actions.

Racism like race is a biocultural phenomenon, produced by real or perceived biological differences interacting with sociocultural factors. English racism toward the Irish was a combination of cultural imperialism and biological determinism. It resulted in the English, as a group, differentially treating the Irish as a group on the basis of biological or social race. However, doctrines of racial superiority are never exclusively biological or sociocultural, for their main purpose was to provide justification for discriminatory behavior.

Sociopolitical conflicts between groups can serve to sharpen and exaggerate even pseudo racial differences between groups. This can create categories of "them" and "us" that encourage racist interactions. As Ashley Montagu once noted:

> "Race in our society is not a term which clearly and dispassionately defines certain real conditions which can be demonstrated to exist but as I have already said, the word acts more as a stimulus which touches off a series of emotional charges that usually bear as much relation to the facts as bees do to bonnets" (Montagu, 1964:118).

Many British political figures from Sir Charles Trevelyan, Assistant Secretary of the Treasury, to Sir Charles Wood, Chancellor of the Exchequer, detested the Irish. Trevelyan said: "The greatest evil we have to face is not the physical evil of the famine but the moral evil of the selfish, perverse and turbulent character of the Irish people." He applauded the fact that starvation encouraged migration. An 1848 article by Trevelyan in the <u>Edinburgh Review</u> supported the view that God was punishing the Irish Catholics for their superstitious ways and adherence to popery. He was knighted that same year for his work on the Famine. Nassau Senior, a British government advisor on economic affairs, actually wished that more might die. The Irish population had been growing at a rate twice that of England, and if organized militarily could have been a threat to British power (Woodham-Smith 1962:374-76). Indeed, without the effects of emigration the population of Ireland would have eventually surpassed that of England and Wales. But perhaps British officials were most troubled by the fact that large numbers of Irish had emigrated to England. In 1841 one out of every 40 persons living in England and Wales was Irish. Ten years later the figure was one in twenty-five, a proportion that presented serious potential for internal strife in the event of a major uprising in Ireland.

In spite of attempts by modern revisionists to soft-pedal the British role in the disaster, quotes from British politicians of the famine period contradict them. Lord

Clarendon, the Lord Lieutenant of Ireland during the starvation, said: "I don't think there is another legislature in Europe that would disregard such suffering as exists in the West of Ireland or coldly persist in a policy of extermination." On resigning his post as Irish Poor Law Commissioner of the Poor Commission, Edward Twistleton said he was an "unfit agent for a policy which would be one of extermination" (Woodham-Smith, 1962).

Britain encouraged emigration to America as a solution. A small number of landlords cleared their estates, by offering their tenants the price of passage to North America. Lord Palmerston, a member of the government, emigrated 2000 Irish from his Sligo estates in 1847. Many were old, sick or widows with children, who arrived naked and were left for charity. The physical condition of Irish immigrants arriving in Canada during "Black 47" was so appalling that the citizens of St. John, New Brunswick and Quebec sent protests to the British Government.

The government refused seed potatoes to those who remained in Ireland, thus allowing the starvation to continue and encouraged further emigration. It would seem that Britain felt that emigration and death would permanently solve the "Irish problem." In this light statements made by leading British statesmen serve to illustrate our point. Lord Russell, the prime minister, noted "... the state of Ireland for the next few months must be one of great suffering ... unhappily the agitation for repeal [of the Act of Union] has contrived to destroy nearly all sympathy in this country." Sir Charles Wood, Chancellor of the Exchequer, once said to Prime Minister Lord Russell that he was "perfectly ready to give as near to nothing as may be."

The British, however, did not deliberately plan the mass death of the Irish people. According to Rubenstein (1983), it would seem that passive genocide is a possible charge for a government that knowingly accepted mass death as a necessary cost associated with their policies. James Donnelly observes that "what happened during and as a result of the clearances had the look of genocide to a great many Irish contemporaries" (1975). From our perspective today, the fact that the British were willing to accept mass death in order to eliminate the Irish peasantry, constitutes genocide. As Doctor Robbie McVeigh has noted,

" The British Government assumed colonial responsibility for the governance of Ireland against the wishes of the vast majority of Irish--yet tolerated the death of 2,000,000 it forcibly made its subjects."

In a book American Holocaust, David Stannard (1995) has argued that natives who died from forced labor, malnutrition, disease, death marches and even despair were victims of genocide. He further suggests that slave labor projects that worked people to death were no less genocidal than direct exterminations. The social dynamics in Ireland that killed or forced the emigration of over 3,000,000 Irish during starvation years certainly fits into Stannard's view of genocide.

The Irish were subjected to a policy of exploitation and destruction with definite physical goals; clearance, death and forced emigration, strategies which some feel were worse than direct genocide. The misery and deprivation of the Irish went on longer. The starvation was not an isolated event, it was an integral part of the continuum of misrule, repression and endemic poverty that characterized British colonial policy. Britain had long range plans for cultural extermination of the Irish, but resistance by the Irish frustrated their attempt. According to Hazel Watters (1993), such resistance facilitated the hardening of anti-Irish racism among the British.

Often the British have explained the starvation in Ireland as a regrettable event that could not be blamed on them. One argument suggests that just as the British accepted the death of troops in wartime, so too should the Irish starvation casualties be accepted. This argument, however, fails to address the fact that the Irish deaths were the result of imperial policy regarding a subjugated nation in peacetime. The rationalization that a money shortage and logistical problems related to a poor transportation system were to blame, does not ring true. Whenever crowds gathered to protest, money and transport for troops to control them were quite adequate. Liz Curtis

(1994) notes that at the end of 1847, after six landlords were killed, an extra 15,000 troops were sent to Ireland.

Another popular British explanation evolved from the misconception that Ireland was overpopulated due to lack of moral restraint, and the fundamental laziness of the Irish people. In other words Irish poverty was their own fault. To the English, the potato unnaturally subsidized the Irish and their large families to the brink of disaster. In the words of geographer, Thomas Freeman: "Apparently content with little the Irish increased and multiplied" (1957:106). Likewise Drake in 1969 noted that "Irish men and women were prepared to live almost exclusively on potatoes." The September 22,1846 Times states:

> "For our own part we regard the potato as a blessing. When the Celts once cease to be potato phagi, they must become carnivorous. With the taste of meats will grow an appetite for them, with the appetite, the readiness to earn them."

By indicating that the potato readily satisfied the primitive needs of the Irish, it depoliticized the poverty of the native Irish, allowing ordinary English people to ignore the abuses of landlordism. The famine was thereby attributed to psychological flaws in the Irish character. The following example, extracted from The London Times, illustrates this point: "The great object of life is to rent a miserable patch of land, to build himself a hovel or burrow in the earth, to marry and if possible to live as well as a pig." Johnathan Pim, Secretary of the Central Relief Committee (Society of Friends) wrote openly of the common racist views held by the British press, and challenged their claims of the Irish character. Here, Pim relates how many Irish people were falsely accused of idleness and improvidence:

> "These vices are attributed by many to the prevalent creed; and their supineness and want of industry are laid at the door of their religion . Others speak of them as the inherent

characteristics of the Celtic race....The inferiority of the Celtic race is a gratuitous assumption, not easy of proof; but even if this be admitted, those who on that account consider the Irish as unimprovable, forget the great admixture of races which has taken place in this country. Most of the maritime cities were Danish colonies" (1848:25).

Malthusian explanations ignore the fact that Irish agricultural output increased steadily in the half century before the starvation. This was true even where the population was increasing the most, yet it did not in any way seem to hurt food production. Also ignored was the reduced socioeconomic status of the native Irish which was the result of land confiscation and policies antagonistic toward Irish culture. Further, the British implemented policies intended to destroy Irish industries. British rule simply hindered all native initiatives and institutions.

O'Grada feels that had the poor been paid better and paid on time for public works the market system might have worked (O'Grada, 1994:197). Recently Christine Kinealy (1995) posited "the response of the British government to the Famine was inadequate in terms of humanitarian criteria and increasingly after 1847 systematically and deliberately so." She feels that if the British had the political will to blunt the starvation they also had the resources to do so. But they wished to use the situation to affect long term agrarian reform at the cost of suffering health, disease, emigration and a legacy of hate and resistance. According to Kinealy the British Government measured the success of Its relief policies by the changes which were imposed on Ireland rather than in the quality of relief provided to their Irish subjects. Food is often used as a weapon of war. It is possible that the British used food as a weapon to bring Ireland to its knees, clear it of multitudes of people and consolidate its political and economic hold on the island.

The British Response

Economics
- No free food while private dealers had it for sale,
- could not undersell dealers

Relief Expenditures
- inadequate especially compared to the buyout of slave holders in 1833

Public Works
- nothing was spent to develop infrastructure   or subsistence
- many were too weak to perform daily physical labor.

Poor Law Amendment, 1847
- because no one with at least ¼ acre was eligible for relief tens of thousands had to give up their land

Soup Kitchens
- after 1847 the only source of aid
- poor quality and not good for bloated, malnourished people

Legal System

- allowed judgements for arrears leading to prison
- so many fled to avoid prosecution

Repeal of Corn Laws, 1848

- used famine as an excuse to repeal; not really meant to help.
  Even if price fell the peasants had no cash to buy grain. Speculators, buying and selling to refief agencies, made a lot of money.

Coercion

- food depots, ships, etc. were guarded by military
- mobile units of 2,000 armed men to deal with food riots

Racism

- Irish viewed as subhuman brutes
- blame the Irish for the starvation, due to psychological flaws
- turned effect into cause

V
Long-Term Effects of the Starvation on Ireland and Britain

On Ireland
The long-term effects of the starvation on Irish agriculture, demography, social organization, including the decline of the Irish language, and Anglo-Irish relations have been immense. According to DeFreine (1965) the famine was a significant factor in the widespread decline of the Irish language. Contributing to this loss was the emigration of national leaders and the discontinued use of Irish by the Catholic church at both diocese and parish level. It has also been noted that after the starvation Irish-speaking parents encouraged their children to abandon Irish in favor of English which was used for all commercial transactions.

Agriculture witnessed a further switch to pasturage, the disappearance of the smaller farms and a great reluctance to divide the farms among one's heirs. Between 1845-1851 the number of plots of one acre or less declined from 493,000 to

280,000. Demographically, the population declined and emigration was institutionalized as a way of life. Between 1845 and 1870 over four million persons left Ireland for other lands, leading to the depopulation of the countryside (Akenson, 1994). The losses were the greatest in the west and the extreme southwest. In some places whole villages disappeared. These include Ballykilcline near Strokestown in County Roscommon, so ably analyzed by Robert Scally in his recent work (1994).

Irish agriculture had experienced a slight trend toward pasturage in the years between 1815 and 1845. The shift was minor in most areas and its short-term effects on the peasant class were somewhat moderated by both emigration and the expansion of tillage onto waste lands. The dramatic switch to grazing was a result of conditions precipitated by the starvation.

Prior to the crisis, local outbreaks of agrarian violence such as the Whiteboys, Defenders and Peep-O-Day Boys, played an important role in limiting evictions and estate consolidation. The Rockite uprising in Munster in the early 1820s had a lasting effect on landlords throughout Ireland long after the Famine of 1822. The strength of secret societies, however, was severely weakened by the starvation and during the late 1840s tens of thousands of families were evicted. Concurrently, the landlords made a large-scale switch to grazing. In the years between 1847 and 1850 the number of cattle in Ireland rose by 327,000.

The livestock industry continued to expand throughout the remainder of the nineteenth century, almost in proportion to the decline in the number of Irish citizens. By the Census of 1861 there were 7,028,000 cattle and sheep grazing on Ireland's pastures. That same year enumerators counted 5,799,000 people, 2,376,000 fewer than census takers found only 20 years earlier. At the turn of the century Irish cattle outnumbered Irish citizens by a slight margin (Mitchell 1992:343).

The trends toward delayed marriage and smaller families, which started as a peasant response to economic change after the Napoleonic Wars, continued in the post-starvation years. Further, an heir had to wait until the father retired in order to inherit the now-indivisible farm. This resulted in a late transfer of status and, often, in the immigration of the young and most vigorous. There are some scholars who do not support the hypothesis that the starvation accelerated these trends. Among the most prominent contemporary scholars is Kevin O'Rourke, who uses computer models to support his alternative stance. He estimates that the monetary drain on Ireland by emigration equalled £35 million annually. In addition, a devotional revolution occurred in Ireland after the starvation which led to a tremendous rise in religious vocations and thus a high rate of celibacy.

A legacy of distrust and hatred influenced Anglo-Irish relations. The folk memory of the ordinary people retains the bitter recollections to this day -- the coffin ships, the soup kitchens, the mass graves, the workhouses; all under the watchful eyes of thousands of well-fed British troops.

A brief rebellion broke out in 1848 but it was doomed from the start. Long on idealism and short on arms, the Young Irelanders were already defeated by two years of starvation and hardship before the first shot was fired. The leadership was too middle class and committed to the sanctity of private property to condone physical violence by the masses. Only John Mitchel and James Fintan Lalor called for open revolt. James Fintan Lalor recognized that Young Ireland was pro-landlord. He opposed O'Connell's Repeal Movement, realizing that breaking the union with Britain did not mean a thing if the people did not control the land. The landlords must go.

> "I acknowledge no right of property which takes the food of millions and gives them famine.... Which denies the peasant the right of home and concedes, in exchange, the right of a workhouse." Lalor in: The Irish Felon, July 8, 1948

Most volunteers had probably hoped as much for food as for freedom, and in their weakened state the small band lost their first and only skirmish to a detachment of policemen.

The Young Irelanders carried the cry of Irish freedom that had passed to them from the risings of 1798 and 1803. The Young Irelanders were possibly the most innovative ideologically of the early Irish rebels, and provided the nationalistic philosophy and literature which served future Irish revolutionaries. Many who emigrated carried the movements to America where it nurtured interest in Irish cultural history, politics and revolution. They passed their ideals along to the Phoenix Society, a group that spawned the Fenian Brotherhood, a world-wide organization of Irish nationalists. The Fenians launched attacks in Canada, Britain and Ireland in 1867, but were defeated on all three fronts. Like those before them, the Brotherhood passed the hope for an independent Ireland to succeeding organizations, such as the Clan na Gael, the Irish Volunteers, the Irish Citizen Army and the Irish Republican Army, who continued to carry on the cause (McCarthy 1883:90-96).

Those Irish who emigrated to the United States formed the basis for a new Irish nation on the opposite side of the Atlantic. The memory of the starvation and coffin ships formed the basis of a deep, enduring hatred of England. It was kept alive through song and story as well as through Irish-American organizations and newspapers. It, along with a litany of further abuses, continues to fuel Irish-American support for an independant Irish Nation.

Impact of the Starvation on Emigration

Mass emigration directly related to the Great Starvation reduced the population of Ireland more than the tragedy of mass death. Between 1845 and 1852 at least 1.5 million Irish citizens left their homeland and permanently resettled in other countries. Aftershocks and chain migration led another 2.5 million out of Ireland by 1870. The general perception of this outpouring of humanity portrays a shift of destitute peasants from rural Ireland to the squalid slums of Anglo-American cities. This over-generalization contains some truths but fails to reveal the full spectrum of Irish emigration between 1845 and 1870. All classes of Irish emigrated, and their experiences varied considerably with respect to cause, economics, route and destination.

Although there are no exact figures regarding Irish emigration, careful examination of the historical record allows estimates which closely approximate the magnitude of the exodus. According to

McVeigh, one-half of the individuals born in Ireland since 1820 have emigrated. Upwards of two million Irish have permanently departed their homeland in the twentieth century, including a vast surge of 500,000 from the Republic of Ireland during the 1950s.

The tradition of leaving Ireland, for political or economic reasons, dates to the 1600s. According to Foster (1988:44) there were 3,000 Irish soldiers in the Spanish Territories by 1614. In 1621 Thomas Nuce offered to plant 2,000 Irish in the New World on behalf of the Virginia Company (Neill 1869:178). By 1700, according to some estimates, five percent of the citizens and soldiers of New France were born in Ireland. Prior to 1700, the largest group of Irish in the New World, however, was composed of thousands of Irish Catholics shipped to Barbados as slaves by Cromwell's order.

Throughout the eighteenth century the exodus of Irish continued to grow as new lands were opened to settlement by European colonial powers. A large proportion of the Irish men and women who emigrated during this century travelled to British North America as indentured servants. Others came as free men and women, eager to make their fortune in the New World. Although there is no accurate tally of the number of Irish who emigrated during the 1700s, archival resources hint at the volume. In 1729 alone, 5,655 Irish arrived at the port of Philadelphia (Holmes in McGee, 1855:25).

The presence of native Irish in colonial America has been underestimated by many historians who attribute the considerable Irish presence solely to the "Scotch-Irish" (O'Brien: 1979). However, the large number of Catholic Irish officers and soldiers in Washington's Continental Army, render this position untenable. The number of ethnic Irish names on Revolutionary War rosters lend further support for an "Irish" presence in Britain's North American colonies. In addition, one must consider the fact that wide use of the term "Scotch-Irish" can be traced to the Native American Movement of the 1840s when it was used by Protestant Irish immigrants who wished to differentiate themselves from their Catholic countrymen. Although Britain's North American possessions received a large proportion of Ireland's emigres, substantial numbers of

Irish settled in other parts of the world.

The Spanish colonies of Argentina and Mexico had significant populations of Irish Catholics by the mid-1700s. A steady trickle of immigrants maintained the Irish presence in these countries for the next century. Thousands more emigrated to Latin America during the starvation. The 1870s saw the movement of more emigrants to Argentina and Mexico in the years following another failure of the potato crop and a resurgence in the rate of evictions. During the decade thousands of Irish men, women and families resettled in these two enclaves. These, in turn, were followed by still more Irish emigrants in the next century, forming the core of current Irish communities in Mexico City and Buenos Aires.

A more significant portion of the exodus chose Australia, and later New Zealand, as their destination. At least 200,000 Irish emigrated to these British colonies between 1845 and 1870. Many were political prisoners or rebels against British rule. It seems likely that a far greater proportion of the Irish would have chosen Australia if the cost of passage had not been four times that of an Atlantic crossing. According to Burchell (1979) a proportion of the Irish who emigrated to Australia later migrated to the United States. A number of those transported to Australia during the starvation eventually settled in the U.S. and Canada. A survey of the Manuscript Census by the authors indicates that many Irish moved from one site to another, often across national borders, before reaching a permanent location.

Irish emigration to Britain and Scotland had a long tradition. This was strengthened by seasonal migration of Irish agricultural workers who depended on employment in the planting and harvest seasons. For many Irish, the tradition became permanent relocation in the years of the Great Starvation. The 1851 Census of Great Britain and Ireland reveals that 6.7 percent of those residing in Scotland in that year had been born in Ireland. That same Census also revealed that more than 400,000 Irish had emigrated to England and Wales during the crisis. The table which appears on page 95 estimates the number of Irish emigrating to England, Scotland and Wales between 1841 and 1850.

The table, based on the number of Irish living in Britain at the 1841 and 1851 Censuses, assumes that the rate of migration across the Irish Sea was one and one-half times that to Canada for the same period. It also presumes an annual mortality rate of 3.1% for these emigrants, a death rate perhaps far below the actual numbers.

It is likely that most of the 362,040 persons who fled to Great Britain between 1845 and 1850 were landless peasants, farm laborers and their families. Fare, which ranged from ten pence in steerage to three pence on deck, could be begged or borrowed. Once ashore in Britain, emigrants were safe from starvation. Soup kitchens, run by charitable organizations in most port cities, dispensed minimal nutrition to the newly-arrived peasants. Most found at least menial work within a short while. Others used Britain as a staging area for step-migration toward a permanent home in the Americas, Australia or elsewhere.

The flow of Irish into England, Scotland and Wales continued after 1850. Unfortunately the London government did not begin keeping records of Irish

IRISH EMIGRATION TO GREAT BRITAIN, 1841-50.

Year	Irish Emigration to Britain	Estimated Irish Immigrant Mortality
1841	36,133	14,007
1842	50,115	15,127
1843	20,367	15,289
1844	24,728	15,582
1845	37,070	16,248
1846	56,833	17,506
1847	147,128	21,524
1848	35,315	21,952
1849	47,798	22,753
1850	37,896	23,223
TOTAL	493,383	183,211

TABLE II

emigration to Great Britain until 1876. Despite this setback, there is sufficient evidence in other documents to make a reasonable approximation of the number of migrants. Table II, above, presupposes that the proportion of Irish emigrants who chose Britain as a destination remained fairly constant from 1850 to 1870. These figures agree with O'Grada (1973) who estimated the net migration to Great Britain between 1852 and 1875 to be at least 730,000 and possibly as high as 810,000 persons.

Akenson (1993:197-200) notes that Irish migrants to Britain were a diverse group. Although the majority of the Irish in cities and towns were poor, there was a significant minority of skilled tradesmen and white collar workers residing in comfortable middle class neighborhoods. The stereotype of the urban slum dweller has perhaps been inappropriately over-emphasized, when the data shows that as late as 1871 only 56.6% of the Irish in England and Wales lived in the 63 largest cities and 16.1% of those resided in London. Estate clearances and chain migration were probably the most important push and pull factors involved in peasant emigration to

Great Britain. Among the other classes of Irish society, the lure of prosperity on the other side of the Irish Sea played a major role in the decision to leave Ireland. But when we calculate the average mortality rates for England, Scotland and Wales between 1851 and 1871, it appears that a substantial number of Irish resided in Britain only long enough to accumulate sufficient capital to continue the journey towards their ultimate destination.

The vast majority of these transmigrants eventually arrived in North America. Canada absorbed about 400,000 Irish immigrants between 1845 and 1870. Further south, the United States drew six times that number in the same era. These figures only approximate the actual number of Irish who sailed to these two countries. No allowance has been made for stowaways, illegal embarkation, or other surreptitious practices, although there are many such references in the historical record.

The voyage from Ireland to America differed greatly from the one day passage to England. Depending on the ship, the weather, and the destination, the trip took as long as three months, and a high percentage of the emigrants perished en route. Once in America, Irish immigrants sent millions of dollars to relatives in Ireland, but only a few ever returned. For many who survived the passage, the memories of the weeks aboard ship deterred any thoughts of re-crossing the Atlantic. Stephen de Vere, a philanthropist who sailed to Canada in steerage during 1847, wrote a horrifying first-hand account of emigrant suffering.

> "Hundreds lay for days like sacks together, quite motionless, with neither light nor air; some were dead; others struck with fever, had no food or medicine other than casual charity; even in delirium they could scarcely turn in their narrow berths" (de Vere in MacDonagh, 1976:411).

Although some ships escaped the ravages of "ship fever" and other crowd-type diseases, the average rate of mortality aboard vessels departing from certain ports indicates the widespread incidence of sickness. In 1847 one out of every nine passengers sailing to North America from Cork died at sea. On

Irish Emigration, 1845-1870

Great Britain:
21,088,087

Australia and New Zealand:
202,708

Ireland

Canada: 399,956

United States:
2,432,643

Latin America:
15,117

Source: Akenson; 1985, 1993

The Irish in the United States, 1850

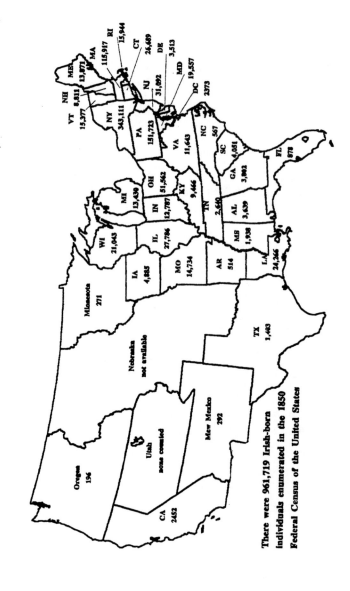

There were 961,719 Irish-born individuals enumerated in the 1850 Federal Census of the United States

ME 13,871
NH 8,811
VT 15,377
MA 115,917
RI 15,944
CT 26,489
NY 343,111
NJ 31,092
PA 151,723
DE 3,513
MD 19,557
DC 2373
VA 11,643
OH 51,562
MI 13,430
IN 12,787
KY 9,466
NC 567
SC 4,051
GA 3,062
FL 878
IL 27,786
WI 21,043
TN 2,650
AL 3,639
MS 1,938
IA 4,885
MO 14,734
AR 514
LA 24,266
Minnesota 271
Nebraska not available
TX 1,443
New Mexico 292
Utah none counted
Oregon 196
CA 2452

100

THE 130th ANNIVERSARY OF THE
GREAT STARVATION
1845 - 1850

IN MEMORY OF THOSE WHO
PERISHED AND THOSE WHO
FLED STARVATION, DEATH AND
FOREIGN OPPRESSION IN
IRELAND TO SEEK JUSTICE, FREEDOM
AND A NEW WAY OF LIFE IN
AMERICA.

❦ ❦ ❦
PRESENTED BY
CLAN NA GAEL OF TOLEDO
- 1995
PRAY FOR THEM

Monument to the Great Starvation

ships departing from Liverpool, the death rate was one in fourteen, and on vessels leaving other Irish ports during that year, one in twenty died. Thousands more arrived sick and died in quarantine. In addition to the immediate deaths, a significant number of emigrants, weakened by famine and the arduous voyage, died within their first year in North America. MacDonagh (1976:410) estimates that "approximately twenty percent of the vast 1847 outflow perished in the attempt to establish themselves on the other shore". Despite the danger and hardship, the flow to North America continued even as the worst of the starvation began to abate. In 1851 nearly a quarter-million Irish boarded ships bound for the Americas.

The Irish came specifically to America in great numbers for a variety of reasons, among which was the encouragement of relatives who had already emigrated. The fact that United States had made a successful and violent break from Britain made the United States more attractive than Canada, where the Irish still had to face British law and prejudice. Fares between Ireland and America were relatively cheap, especially if one travelled on a commercial ship which was returning to the United States after delivering raw materials to British manufacturers. In these cases emigrants could get cheap transport as sort of "paying ballast." American vessels also had a better reputation for the treatment of passengers. However, the reputation of the United States as a land of freedom and opportunity was probably the greatest reason for coming to "Amerikay"[*].

Traditionally, historians have placed the majority of Irish immigrants in the squalid ethnic ghettoes situated on the least desirable real estate of major American cities. Census data published by the U.S. and Canadian governments appears to support these claims if one examines the cross-tabulations concerning nativity and location. Further investigation involving the original manuscripts indicates that although a high percentage of Irish immigrants can be found in urban areas, many individuals resided in a given city for only a limited time. Irishmen who were counted in the New York

---

[*]A corruption of the Gaelic word for America.

Census of 1850 can be found scattered across the United States in the 1860 Census.

While the number of Irish living in major cities remained high, the statistics reveal nothing about the continuous inflow and exodus that occurred among the migrants. The replacement immigrants continued to occupy many of the jobs at the low end of the occupational ladder, contributing to the stereotype. At this point, in-depth studies of families and individuals suggest that a large proportion of Irish immigrants used the cities as a stepping stone on the path back to a more rural lifestyle in the interior of the continent.

The United States did not welcome the Irish with open arms. Many resented their arrival and tried to stop or discourage the flow of emigrants. The Irish in the United States were initially subject to poverty, prejudice and outright threats to their life and well being. Irish neighborhoods were attacked, churches burned and individuals assaulted and killed. There were attempts to prevent the Irish from gaining employment as witnessed by the "No Irish Need Apply" signs, which were common.

Irish-Americans in 1990

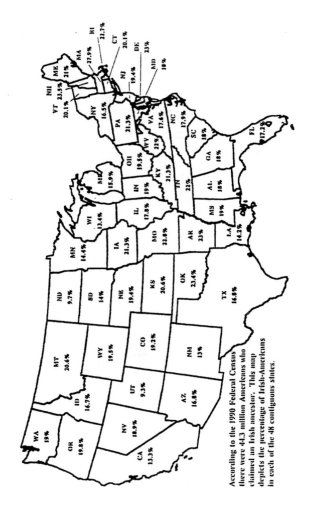

According to the 1990 Federal Census there were 44.3 million Americans who claimed an Irish ancestor. This map depicts the percentage of Irish-Americans in each of the 48 contiguous states.

Irish fought back and made the most of what opportunities were afforded them. With the passage of time they gradually moved from low-paid, unskilled jobs to better-paid more stable occupations and professions. In fact the Irish eventually became one of the most successful of all immigrant groups. The Irish, however, did not succeed because American society was open, but rather because America had an expanding economy with almost unlimited job opportunities. The Irish, given the opportunity to advance themselves, willingly accepted employment in all sectors of the American economy.

The Irish, along with African Americans and Asian Americans, supplied much of the unskilled labor required to build the infrastructure so essential to the industrialization of the United States after the Civil War. It was the Irish who built many canals, sewers, water systems, railroads and roadways necessary for both urbanization and industrialization. One author said that the United States ran on steam power, water power and Irish power.

The Great Starvation had far reaching effects on the history of the United States.

The Irish immigrants of this time period were possibly the most assertively Irish and the least culturally Catholic to date. They were willing to aggressively challenge the Anglo-American for their rights. Many of these immigrants who settled in well-defined urban areas, contributed to both the urbanization of America and the growth of urban machine politics.

The Irish used the knowledge of the Anglo system of government that they had learned in Ireland during the struggle for emancipation and repeal to gain a foothold in American politics. The Irish didn't invent the big city political machine but they certainly improved its function and power. They did, however, use their neighborhoods as an initial power base in delivering votes for the Democratic Party until eventually the Irish gained control of the party locally, and with it control of city after city. They became the masters of the coalition politics which held together the Democratic Party with its diverse, often desperate, elements. This coalition held together until the anti-ethnic McGovern group took over the party in 1972. Many Irish American responded to insults and the insensitivity of the McGovernites by defecting en masse to the Republican Party during the 1970s and 80s.

The large influx of Irish in the last half of the nineteenth century changed the American Catholic Church from a quiet, reserved institution to an aggressive growth oriented organization. Irish Catholics established and constructed numerous parishes and instituted the beginnings of the parochial school system in America. The Irish left a lasting imprint on the nature of the American Catholic Church, with their bricks and mortar approach to expansion. They were also an important element in the development of Catholic-oriented social welfare institutions, including systems of hospitals and orphanages.

The Irish were also consistent supporters of the American theory of expansionism known as Manifest Destiny. Traditionally, the Irish and Irish American component of American society has supplied a disproportionate number of its offspring to the armed forces. They have been a significant segment of the U.S. military from the American Revolution to the Vietnam War. In fact, they have been an important factor in the growth and development of the United

States military at all ranks and in all capacities.

The Great Starvation also helped to establish an Irish nation in America that would oppose British control of their native land. Irish American nationalism fed on memories of poverty, starvation, forced emigration and the degradation and social debilitation imposed upon the Irish people by British colonialism. Irish American organizations and the Irish American press cultivated antagonism toward Ireland's oppressors that has lasted until the present day. "Revenge for Skibbereen" can still be heard at rallies and gatherings among Irish American political activists.

In 1860, The London Times, quoted a British politician who was disturbed by the mass migration of the Irish to the United States:

"If this exodus goes on as it is likely to go on, the United States will become very Irish. So, an Ireland there will still be, but on a colossal scale and in a New World. We shall only have pushed the Celt westwards, then no longer cooped up between the Liffey and the Shannon, he will spread from New York to San Francisco and keep up the ancient feud at an unforeseen advantage. We must gird our loins to encounter the nemesis of s e v e n c e n t u r i e s o f misgovernment. Till the end of time a hundred million Celts spread over the largest habitable area in the world and, confronting us everywhere by sea and land, will remember that their forefathers paid tithe to the Protestant clergy, rent to the absentee landlords, and a forced obedience to the laws which they had made."

VI
Holocaust or Revisionist Whitewash

Mary Daly in her book, <u>The Famine in Ireland</u>, attempts to mitigate British culpability with respect to starvation in Ireland, concluding that "it does not appear appropriate to pronounce in an unduly critical fashion on the limitations of previous generations." Roy Foster in his landmark revisionist work <u>Modern Ireland 1600-1972</u>, downplays the famine as a watershed in Irish history and presents it in a very sanitized manner, devoid of any humanistic consideration. He even informs us that Irish landlords charged low rents and rarely evicted their tenants. These two works are symptomatic of the perversion of historical reality in Ireland today. Discussion of the famine period has even been eliminated from many school curricula. Cecil Woodham-Smith, the Oxford-trained historian who wrote the influential work, <u>The Great Hunger</u>, is dismissed as too populist, simplistic and emotional to suit academic historians.　J.M. Goldstrom (1981) has whined "too many writers of Irish history have permitted the plight of the starving peasant to determine their perspectives...on the Great Famine."

Australian Patrick O'Farrell has called the starvation "a revolution" since it ended the peasant society, and claimed that the nationalist response was counter-revolutionary. He also claims that: "It is difficult to disentangle the realities of the response of the Irish peasant...from the contrary overlays imposed by aggressive nationalist writing" (O'Farrell, 1984). O'Farrell's viewpoints on the ethos of the Irish peasantry rely heavily on the writings of Mrs. Elizabeth Smith, an English landowner who recorded her observations in her Irish journals. His position is the antithesis of John Mitchel, an Irishman who revisionist historians see as the alpha and omega of the nationalist view of the starvation.

Terence Duffy of Magee College says that Luke Dodd of the Strokestown Famine Museum would rather view the starvation as an event that happened for a peculiar set of circumstances rather than the result of any particular policies. Duffy hopes the Famine

Museum will not portray the Irish as victims. He feels we must escape from the "imprisonment" of Irish traditional perspectives. Doctor Duffy, a human rights specialist, apparently has little appreciation for the history of human rights abuse.

In 1861 in <u>The Last Conquest of Ireland</u>, John Mitchell wrote:

> "The Almighty indeed sent the potato blight but the English created the famine." Mitchel further observed that "a million and half men, women and children were carefully, prudently and peacefully slain by the English Government. They died of hunger in the midst of abundance which their own hands created."

Such sentiment expressed by an Irishman who witnessed the horrors inflicted upon his countrymen will always linger, refuting revisionist attempts to obscure reality.

Irish academic analysis has in recent years been dominated by planned counter-revolutionary or neo-colonialist revision of the historical record. It would appear that one of the major purposes of the rewriting of Irish history is to undermine the basis of Irish nationalism and leave Ireland without heroes or historical memory. It also plays down the British responsibility for the catastrophic aspects of the Irish experience. They have created the impression that death was inevitable, inadvertent or the intended consequences of a tragic event. Though they alternately whimper or crow about their quest for detached truth, Anglo-Irish revisionists attempt to present sociopolitical propaganda under the guise of scholarly writing. They choose to forget that British rule in Ireland was guided by the rope and the bayonet.

Even non-historians realize that revision of history is a necessity as new facts and potentially valid reinterpretations of events, personalities and trends become apparent. Many historians, however, write from the point of view of the powerful or the acceptable intellectual paradigms of the day and not the experience of ordinary people, especially the oppressed. This is very common among historian writing about British ruled Ireland. Reading historians such as Francis Godwin James (<u>Ireland in the Empire - 1688-1770</u>) one gets the idea that the only "Irish" worthy of notice were the Anglo-Irish ruling class in Dublin! The huge, silent majority of Gaelic Irish are just not mentioned. These were the famine victims.

Social and political elites who control the media, the universities and publishing outlets prefer writers who support and comfort them in their position of privilege, and add further to their power and prestige. As Edward Said (1979) has said, approved histories employ "the moral epistemology of imperialism" and attempt the "blotting out of knowledge" of the collective memory of the indigenous people. In Ireland, revisionism is fueled by academic paranoia with regard to the politics of Irish nationalism today. Christine Kinealy, in an interview in the <u>Chicago Tribune</u>, said that one historian tried to talk her out of writing on the starvation because she would give "ideological bullets to the IRA." As Cormac O'Grada (1994) has noted, it's as "if we tell them what happened during the Famine they will all join the IRA". He also chides scholars like Mary Daley for using the "language of academic fright." Further, one reviewer observed that Trevelyan will never die as long as Mary Daly lives with her parallel interpretation of the starvation. As historians, they know full well that the unaltered history of Anglo-Irish relations stands on its own merits as the foundation for the sociohistorical validity of modern Irish republicanism. It, therefore, behooves revisionists to reinterpret the British role in the history of Ireland so that their sociocultural idols do not look so bad. They also treat us to a heavy dose of blaming the victim. Furthermore, where were the protests of Irish academics with respect to the obscene socioeconomic status of many nationalists in the six counties; the perverted system of justice both North and South; the murder of the Irish people by the British army, the RUC and loyalist death squads; and the implementation of the draconian Section 31 censorship? Elitism and irrelevance, however, are often characteristic of academia on both sides of the Atlantic.

Self-aggrandizing individuals, of whatever ilk, do not exhibit the communalistic values necessary to take a position on the side of social justice. Irish universities, according to Robbie McVeigh

(1995:12): "... show little more concern for the needs of the poorest and most oppressed sectors of the community in contemporary Ireland." In 1981 Bobby Sands and his comrades demonstrated with their own lives that there are values beyond egoism, materialism and sanctimonious moralism worth dying for. We would also like to remind Irish academics that were it not for the men and women of violence in 1916-21, they and their colleagues would possibly be practicing their craft as tour guides in English country houses.

In a review, Andrew Greeley blamed Foster's style on the intellectual climate in Britain. But, we would suggest that the neocolonial mentality of a significant portion of Irish academia is to blame -- a mentality that makes them want to be Europeans because they know that their pompous English role models will not let them be English. Colonialism in the Caribbean produced Afro-Saxons, in Ireland it produced West Britons. In The Colonizer and the Colonized, Memmi noted that groups emerged to mimic the oppressors. Universities in Ireland are a memorial to the after effects of colonialism in Ireland. In

Cork, university authorities have ressurected their statue of the "Famine Queen", Victoria, and display it as part of the activities associated with the 150th anniversary of the university's founding. This is a truly arrogant display of insensitivity to their heritage as well as clearly illustrating the ongoing survival of colonial mentality.

Revisionists might do well by heeding the words of Donal McCartney, the distinguished UCD professor of history: "... and then nothing can be more unhistorical or unprofessional then when the revisionist stands by the gallows or beside the firing squad and curses the victims as they pass." Professor Kevin Whelan (1995) claims that an unnatural symbiotic relationship has existed between the revisionist scholar, the popular media and much of the political establishment in Ireland.

British Member of Parliament Ken Livingstone, in 1984, caused an uproar in Britain by comparing Britain's treatment of the starving Irish with that of Hitler's treatment of the Jews in World War II. He also charged that Britain tried to commit genocide in Ireland and has been rewriting its Irish and British history ever since. His remarks were vigorously challenged by the British press and many English letter-writers called him a "lying traitor." One writer even suggested that only 20,000 died and the rest emigrated and did not die on the roads as the Irish claimed. Recent research, however, reveals that at least ten times that figure, perhaps more than a quarter million Irish victims of the Great Starvation, are buried in unmarked graves. Across the Atlantic, in the United States, most writers acknowledge the excessive deaths caused by the Starvation. A 1982 article in relatively conservative Journal of the National Geographic Society claimed that "in Ireland six ghastly years of famine led to a million deaths (Rhoades, 1982:679)."

British apologists would do well to ponder the words of the great British writer William Makepiece Thackeray who characterized British colonialism in Ireland as follows:

"... It is a frightful document against ourselves ... one of the most melancholy stories in the whole world of insolence, rapine, brutal, endless slaughter and persecution on the part of the English master; ... There is no crime ever invented by eastern or western barbarians, no torture or Roman persecution or Spanish Inquisition, no tyranny of Nero or Alva but can be matched in the history of England in Ireland." (Thackery, 1846)

It is time for us to stop using the euphemism "Irish Potato Famine" for two reasons. First, it is wrong because there was no shortage of food in Ireland. Secondly, it was not simply an "Irish famine" but a starvation based on systematic British exploitation of the Irish people, inaction in the face of the potato crop failure and a vindictive, racist attitude toward the Irish.

The events of 1845-1850 were truly a holocaust. Indeed, in 1904 Michael Davitt, the founder of the Irish Land League, called it a holocaust. It is not something for the Irish and Irish Americans to forget. Why is it that the Irish are told to stop living in the past or that they have too long a memory? Would anyone ask Jews to forget the Nazi atrocities against their people? Should

Native Americans forget the massacres at Sand Creek and Wounded Knee? Would we suggest that African Americans forget the horrors of the middle passage? How can we learn from the past if we are ignorant of its successes, failures and abominations? Elie Wiesel once said that "the danger lies in forgetting. Forgetting, however, will not only effect the dead. Should it trample the ashes of yesterday, it will cover our hopes for tommorrow" (Rothschild, 1981).

In the words of the Irish patriot labor leader James Connolly, "The English administration of Ireland during the famine was a colossal crime against the human race." We should not forget our holocaust orchestrated by English imperialists and we should not let the world forget. In August 1989, during an address on Grosse Ile, Canada, Dr. Edward J. Brennan, Ireland's ambassador to Canada, noted: "The Great Famine was Ireland's holocaust (which) condemned the Irish to be the first boat people of modern Europe" (Quigley, 1994:55).

We should dare not forget the terrible death and suffering that stalked Ireland between 1845 and 1850. In fact, we should indelibly fix it in our personal and collective memory for we are our ancestors. Terry Eagleton, a philosopher, has written: "The Irish cannot forget their history because the English refuse to remember it" (Moseley, 1995).

Illustrated London News

Death Wagons in County Cork

Bibliography

Akenson, Donald H. 1984. The Irish in Ontario: A Study in Rural History. McGill-Queen's University Press, Kingston, Ontario.

_____. 1985. Being Had: Historians, Evidence, and the Irish to North America. P.D. Meany, Port Credit, Ontario.

_____. 1993. The Irish Diaspora: A Primer. P.D. Meany, Streetsville, Ontario.

Brown, Malcolm. 1972. The Politics of Irish Literature From Thomas Davis to W.B. Yeats. University of Washington Press, Seattle, WA.

Burchell, Robert A. 1979. The San Francisco Irish, 1848-1880. Manchester University Press, Manchester, England.

Candaele, K. and K. Candaele. 1994. "Revisionists and the Writing of Irish History." Irish America, July/August, 1994:22-27.

Campbell, P. 1994. "Remembering the Great Hunger at Home and Abroad." Irish Echo, Jan, 4, 1994. p. 25.

_____. 1995. Death in Templecrone. Templecrone Press, Jersey City, NJ.

Commissioner of Agriculture. 1888. Section of Vegetable Pathology, Plate I (Phytophthora Infestans). In: Report of the Commissioner of Agriculture. Government Printing Office, Washington, DC.

Connell, K. 1962. "The Potato in Irish History." Past and Present, 23:57-71.

Coote, C. 1801. General View of Agriculture and Manufacturers of King's County. Graisberry and Campbell, Dublin.

124

Corrigan, D.J. 1846. On Famine and Fever As Cause and Effect in Ireland. J. Fennin, Dublin.

Cousens, S.H. 1960. "Regional Birth Rates in Ireland During the Great Famine from 1846-1854." Population Studies, 14:1:55-74.

Crawford, M. ed. 1989. Famine: The Irish Experience 900-1900. John Donald Publishing, Edinburgh.

Curtis, Liz. 1994. The Cause of Ireland: From United Irishmen to Partition. Beyond the Pale: Belfast.

Daly, Mary E. 1986. The Famine in Ireland. Dublin Historical Association, Dundalgan Press, Dublin.

De Bow, J.D.B. 1853. Seventh Census of the United States, 1850. Robert Armstrong, Washington, DC.

DeFreine, S. 1965. The Great-Silence. Mercier Press, Dublin. pp. 66-74.

Donnelly, J.S. 1975. <u>The Land and the People of Nineteenth Century Cork</u>. Routledge and Kegan Paul, London.

_____. 1995. "Historians and the Famine Debate." <u>Irish Echo</u>, March 15-21; p. 37.

Drake, M. 1969. <u>Population Growth and the Irish Economy</u> In: <u>The Formation of the Irish Economy</u>. L. Cullen ed. Mercier Press, Cork. pp. 65-70.

Duffy, T. 1996. The Museum of the Irish Famine: Exhibiting Ireland's Tragic History. <u>Museum International</u>, 190:251-53.

<u>Economist, The</u>. 1853. "Effects of Emigration on Production and Consumption." <u>The Economist</u>, 2:494:168-169.

Edwards, R.D. and T.D. Williams, eds. 1957. <u>The Great Famine: Studies in Irish History 1845-52</u>. New York University Press, New York.

Foster, Robert Fitzroy. 1988. Modern Ireland: 1600-1972. Penguin Press: New York.

Freeman, T. 1957. Pre-Famine Ireland: A Study in Historical Geography. Manchester University Press, Manchester.

Gallagher, T. 1982. Paddy's Lament. Harcourt Brace, New York.

Gibbon, P. 1975. "Colonialism and the Great Starvation in Ireland 1845-1849." Race and Class, 17:2:131-139.

Goldstrom, J.M. 1981. "Irish Agriculture and the Great Famine." In: Irish Population Economy and Society. J.M. Goldstrom and L.A. Clarkson, eds. Oxford University Press, Oxford. pp. 155-172.

Kennedy, R.E.J. 1973. The Irish: Emigration, Marriage and Fertility. University of California, Berkley.

127

Kinealy, C. 1995. <u>The Great Calamity: The Irish Famine 1845-1852</u>. Gill and Macmillan, Dublin.

<u>Illustrated London News</u>. 1845-1852. London.

Lebow, R.N. 1976. <u>White Britain and Black Ireland: The Influence of Stereotypes on Colonial Policy</u>. Institute for the Study of Human Issues, Philadelphia.

_____. 1977. "British Images of Poverty in Pre Famine Ireland." In: <u>Views of the Irish Peasantry 1800-1916</u>. D.J. Casey and R.E. Rhodes eds. Archon, Hamdan, CT. pp. 57-85.

Lees, J.H. and J. Modell. 1977. "The Irish Countryman Urbanized: A Comparative Perspective on Famine Migration." <u>Journal of Urban History</u>, 34:391-408.

Lalor, J.F. 1848. <u>The Irish Felon</u>. July 8, 1848.

<u>The London Times</u>. September 22, 1846.

Lysaght, P. 1986. "Continuity and Change in Irish Diet." In: Food in Change. A. Fenton and E. Kisban eds. John Donald Publishing, Glasgow.

MacDonagh, Oliver. 1976. "The Irish Famine Emigration to the United States." Perspectives in American History, X:355-446.

McCarthy, Justin H. 1883. An Outline of Irish History from Earliest Times to the Present Day. John W. Lovell, New York.

McDowell, R.B. 1957. "Ireland on the Eve of Famine." In: The Great Famine: Studies in Irish History 1845-1852. R.D. Edwards and T.D. Williams eds. New York University Press, New York.

McGee, Thomas D'Arcy. 1855. A History of the Irish Settlers in North America, from the Earliest Period of the Census of 1850. Sixth Ed. Patrick Donahoe: Boston.

McVeigh, R. 1995. "The Last Conquest of Ireland: British Academics in Irish Universities." Race and Class, 37:1:109-121.

_____. no date. Hunger: An Gorta Mor. Centre for Research and Documentation, Belfast.

Memmi, A. 1965. The Colonizer and the Colonized. Orion Books, New York.

Mitchel, J. 1873. The Crusade of the Period And Last Conquest of Ireland (Perhaps). Lunch, Cole and Meehan, New York.

Mitchell, B.R. 1992. International Historical Statistics: Europe, 1750-1988. Stockton Press, New York.

Mokyr, J. 1985. Why Ireland Starved?: A Quantitative and Analytical History of the Irish Economy 1800-1845. Allen & Unwin, London.

Montagu, A.M.F. 1964. <u>Mans Most Dangerous Myth: The Fallacy of Race</u>. World Publishing, Cleveland, Ohio.

Morgan, V. 1976. "A Case Study of Population Change Over Two Centuries: Blaris, Lisburn 1661-1848." <u>Irish Economic and Social History</u>, 3:5-16.

Moseley, R. 1995. "Famine Still Pains Irish." <u>Chicago Tribune</u>, July 30, 1995, Section 1:13,16.

Muligan, H.A. 1995. "Living With the Ghosts of the Potato Famine." <u>Detroit News</u>, July, 1995.

<u>The Nation</u>. October 16, 1847.

Neill, Edward D. 1869. <u>History of the Virginia Company</u>. Joel Munsell, New York.

Newenham. 1805. <u>A Statistical and Historical Inquiry into the Progress and Magnitude of the Republic of Ireland</u>. C & R Baldwin, London.

O'Brien, M.J. 1979. <u>Irish Settlers in America</u>. Geneaological Publishing Co., Baltimore.

O'Brien, W.P. 1896. <u>The Great Famine in Ireland</u>. Downes, London.

O'Connor F. 1967. <u>The Backward Look: A Survey of Irish Literature</u>. Macmillan, London.

O'Donovan, J. 1940. <u>The Economic History of Livestock in Ireland</u>. Cork University Press, Cork.

O'Farrell. 1982. "Whose Reality?: The Irish Famine in History and Literature." <u>Historical Studies</u>, 20:1013.

O'Grada, Cormac. 1973. "A Note on Nineteenth Century Irish Emigration Statistics". <u>Population Studies</u>, 29:143-49.

_____. 1988. <u>Ireland Before and After the Famine: Explorations in Economic Theory 1800-1925</u>. Manchester University, Manchester.

_____. 1989. The Great Irish Famine. Macmillan Press, London.

_____. 1994. From Ireland: A New Economic History 1780-1939. Clarendon Press, London. pp. 175-200.

O'Neill, T.P. 1957. "The Organization and Administration of Relief in 1845-1852." In: The Great Famine: Studies in Irish History 1845-1852. R.D. Edwards and T.D. Williams eds. New York University Press, New York.

O'Rourke, J. 1902. "History of the Great Irish Famine of 1847." Duffy, Dublin.

O'Rourke, K. 1991. Did the Great Irish Famine Matter? Journal of Economic History, 51:1:1-22.

Parliamentary Papers, 1847-48. Papers relating to...relief of distress. Vol. 55:467-68. 15th Series.

Pim, J. 1848. The Condition and Prospects of Ireland and the Evils Arising From the Present Distribution of Landed Property with Suggestion for a Remedy, 1848. Hodges and Smith, Dublin.

Quigley, M. 1994. "Grosse Ile: An Argument and Some Modest Proposals." Canadian Journal of Irish Studies, 20:1:41-59.

Rhoades, Robert E. 1982. "The Incredible Potato." National Geographic, 161:5:668-94.

Ross, E. 1985. "Potatoes, Population and the Irish Famine: The Political Economy of Demographic Change." In: Culture and Reproduction: Reconstructing the Demographic Paradigm. Handwerker ed. Westview Press, Boulder, Colo. pp. 81-104.

Rothschild, S., ed. 1981. Voices from the Holocaust. New American Library, New York.

Rubenstein, R.L. 1983. "The Irish Famine." In: The Age of Triage. R.L. Rubenstein. Beacon Press, Boston. pp. 98-127.

Said, E. 1979. The Question of Palestine. Times Books, New York.

Scally, R.J. 1994. The End of Hidden Ireland: Rebellion, Famine and Emigration. Oxford, New York.

Smith, A. 1937. The Wealth of Nations. Random House, New York.

Stannard, D.E. 1992. American Holocaust: Columbus at the Conquest of the New World. Oxford University Press, New York.

Thackery, W.M. 1846. "Moore's History of Ireland: From the Earliest Kings of that Realm Down to Its Last Chief." 4 vols. Reprinted in The Morning Chronicle, August 20, 1846.

Watters, H. 1995. "The Great Famine and the Rise of Anti-Irish Racism." <u>Race and Class</u>, 37:1:95-108.

Whelan, K. 1995. Pre and Post Famine Landscape Change. In: <u>The Great Irish Famine</u>. C. Poiter, ed. Mercier, Cork. pp. 19-33.

Woodham-Smith, C. 1962. <u>The Great Hunger</u>. Harper and Row, New York.

Young, A. 1780. <u>A Tour of Ireland: With General Observations on the Present Statement of the Kingdom: Made in the Years 1776, 1777, 1778 and Brought Down to the End of 1779</u>. 2 vols. H. Goldney, London.

Appendix A

NOTRE DAME LAW SCHOOL
Notre Dame, Indiana 46556

DIAL DIRECT NUMBER:
(219) 631-5667

February 20, 1996

Mr. Owen Rodgers
Irish Famine/Genocide Committee
c/o O'Dwyer & Bernstien
52 Duane St.
New York, NY 10007

Dear Mr. Rodgers:

You asked my opinion on whether the Irish Famine was genocide. In my opinion it was genocide.

The Genocide Convention, Article II, provides:

> In the present Convention, genocide means any of the following acts committed with intent to destroy, in whole or in part, a national, ethnical, racial or religious group, as such:
>
>> (a) Killing members of the group;
>>
>> (b) Causing serious bodily or mental harm to members of the group;
>>
>> (c) Deliberately inflicting on the group conditions of life calculated to bring about its physical destruction in whole or in part;
>>
>> (d) Imposing measures intended to prevent births within the group;
>>
>> (e) Forcibly transferring children of the group to another group.

The actions of the British Government during the Famine clearly demonstrated the requisite intent and clearly fit within the criteria at least of subdivisions (a), (b) and (c) of Article II.

The Irish Famine provided a model for the many and varied episodes of genocide which followed over the succeeding 150 years. And we are not done with the pattern of genocide yet. If the people of the world are to reverse that pattern, an important first step will be for the world community to condemn the engineered oppression of the Irish people by the British government during the Famine. The British policies with respect to the Famine reached a height, or depth, of deliberate indifference to innocent life, which is utterly reprehensible and not exceeded in any subsequent genocide.

Sincerely,

Charles E. Rice
Professor of Law

137

Appendix B
Selected Readings:
Revisionist and Post Revisionist

Campbell, P. 1995. <u>Death in Templecrone:</u> <u>An Account of the Famine Years in</u> <u>Northwest Donegal 1845-1850</u>. Templecrone Books, New Jersey.

Cowman, D. and D. Brady. 1995. <u>The</u> <u>Famine in Waterford 1845-50</u>. Geography Publications, Dublin.

Daly, M.E. 1986. <u>The Famine in Ireland</u>. Dublin Historical Association, Dundalgan, Press, Dublin.

Donnelly, J.S. 1975. <u>The Land and People</u> <u>of Nineteenth Century Cork</u>. Routledge and Kegan Paul, London.

Edwards, R.D. and T.D. Williams, ed. 1957. <u>The Great Famine: Studies in Irish</u> <u>History 1845-52</u>. New York University Press, New York.

Gallagher, T. 1982. Paddy's Lament. Harcourt Press, New York.

Garner, E. 1986. To Die By Inches: The Famine in Northeast Cork. Eigse Books, Fermoy, Cork.

Gray, P. 1996. Famine, Land and Politics: British Government and Irish Society, 1843-1850. Irish Academic Press, Dublin.

Kelleher, M. 1996. The Feminization of Famine: Representations of Women in Famine Narratives. Cork University Press, Cork, Ireland.

Kierse, S. 1984. The Famine Years in the Parish of Killaloe 1845-1851. Boru Books, Killaloe, County Clare.

Killen, J., ed. 1995. The Famine Decade: Contemporary Accounts 1841-1851. The Blackstaff Press, Belfast.

Kinealy, C., S. Cannon and S. Cox. 1992. The Famine in Dunfanaghy. Dublin.

Kinealy, C. 1995. The Great Calamity: The Irish Famine 1845-1852. Gill & Macmillan, Dublin.

McKay, D. 1990. Flight From Famine: The Coming of the Irish to Canada. McCleeland and Stewart, Toronto.

Mokyr, J. 1985. Why Ireland Starved: A Quantitative and Analytical History of the Irish Economy 1800-1845. Allen & Unwin, London.

Morash, C. and R. Hayes, ed. 1996. Fearful Realities: An Introduction. Irish Academic Press, Dublin.

Murphy, I. 1996. A Starving People: Life and Death in West Clare, 1845-1851. Irish Academic Press, Dublin.

O'Brien, W.P. 1896. The Great Famine in Ireland. Downes, London.

O'Connor, J. 1995. The Workhouses of Ireland: The Fate of Ireland's Poor. Anvil Books, Dublin.

O'Gallagher, M. 1984. Grosse Ile: Gateway to Canada 1832-1957. Carraig Books, Ste. Foy, Quebec.

O'Gallagher, M. and R.M. Dompierre. 1995. Eyesitness: Grosse Isle, 1847. Carraig Books, Ste. Foy, Quebec.

O'Grada, C. 1989. The Great Irish Famine. Macmillan, London.

O'Rourke, J. 1874. The Great Irish Famine. Veritas Publ., Dublin (1989 reprint).

Poirteir, C. 1995. Famine Echoes. Gill & Macmillan, Dublin.

Poirteir, C., ed. 1995. The Great Irish Famine. Mercier Publishing.

Rees, J. 1994. A Farewell to Famine. Arklow Enterprise Center, Arklow, Ireland.

Scally, R.J. 1994. The End of Hidden Ireland: Rebellion, Famine and Emigration. Oxford, New York.

Scott, T.C. 1853. Connemora After the Famine: Journal of a Survey of the Martin Estate 1853. Reprinted & ed. T. Robinson, Dublin, 1995.

Shell, K.M., ed. 1995. Letters From Ireland During the Famine of 1847. (by Alexander Somerville) Irish Academic Press, Dublin.

United States Congress. 1854. Report of the Select Committee of the Senate of the United States on the Sickness and Mortality on Board Emigrant Ships. Beverley Tucker, Senate Printer, Washington, D.C. (1977 Reprint Edition by Arno Press, New York)

Woodham-Smith, C. 1962. The Great Hunger. Harper & Row, New York.

Appendix C

The Great Hunger:
TIME FOR AN ENGLISH APOLOGY

The great British writer William Makepeace Thackeray described English colonial rule in Ireland as follows:

> *"It's a frightful document against ourselves -- one of the most melancholy stories in the whole world of insolence, rapine, brutal, endless slaughter, and persecution. There is no crime ever invented by eastern or western barbarians, no torture or Roman persecution or Spanish Inquisition, no tyranny of Nero or Alva but can be matched in the history of the English in Ireland."*

The American Ireland Education Foundation-PEC has commenced a grassroots campaign to seek from the British government an apology for causing much of the death and suffering during Ireland's Great Hunger. We need your help to make this campaign a success.

An English apology must be one of the goals of the Irish American community during the 5-year commemoration (September 1995 through September 2000) of the 150th anniversary of the Great Hunger. This man-made starvation claimed up to 2 million lives and forced another 2 million Irish to emigrate. Between 1845 and 1850, Ireland lost half its population. Yet, during the potato blight, England shipped out of Ireland enough food to feed the population twice over.

Such an apology would be in keeping with other worldwide reconciliation efforts. The Southern Baptist Church in America has apologized to black people for their past support of slavery. Germany has apologized to the Jewish race for Nazi atrocities. Japan apologized for wartime abuses against Korean women. These are wise international healing gestures. Now, as we commemorate the Great Hunger, an English apology would be an appropriate gesture.

Reputable scholars now recognize that rigid English adherence to *laissez-faire* principles of political economy, lack of sympathy with the Irish people and outright anti-Irish hostility converted the tragedy of the potato blight into a disaster. Why not an apology by the English?

An English apology is long overdue the Irish people. The first step toward reconciliation, which would demonstrate the sincerity of the British government, would be to acknowledge responsibility for the magnitude of the disaster. An apology would be the stroke which starts to melt the hard blocking movement to bring peace with justice to Northern Ireland.

PEC has commenced the campaign by writing to the British government requesting an apology.

The British government's acknowledging responsibility for the Great Hunger is important to today's English-Irish peace process. The British portray themselves as impartial brokers in Ireland keeping peace between Catholics and Protestants. Yet history shows they are responsible for fomenting dissent among the Irish people and for supporting the loyalists' pro-Union position. By acknowledging responsibility for the neglect that caused the famine, we hope the British will acknowledge their partiality in Irish affairs and, therefore, accept the need for an impartial negotiator to broker the settlement in Ireland.

People like you have a major role to play in making this just campaign a success--as you did with the Boston College-Thatcher campaign. **The campaign must continue until the British government acknowledges its responsibility.** This means that you can hand out this R&D throughout the 5-year duration of the commemoration. We can obtain an English apology, **but only with your help.** Get others to assist you.

HOW YOU CAN HELP

1. Write the letter below to: British Ambassador John Kerr, British Embassy, 3100 Massachusetts Avenue, N.W., Washington, DC 20008.

Dear Mr. Kerr:

In commemoration of the 150th anniversary of Ireland's Great Hunger, please urge the British government to issue an apology to the Irish people in acknowledgment of responsibility for this enormous calamity. Such an acknowledgment is essential to establishing peace and reconciliation in Ireland.

2. Send a copy of this PEC *Reproduce & Distribute* (R&D) to all Irish American organizations and the different new media (newspapers, radio & TV news programs, college media, etc.) in your community. Distribute them at dances, *feisanna*, festivals, concerts, etc. Mail them to friends, relatives, etc. throughout the U.S. and abroad.

147

Petition Campaign

3. PEC is petitioning the British prime minister for an apology for the neglect that caused the Great Hunger. Readers in the US and abroad can get copies from us, photocopy them, get them signed, and return them to us so we can deliver them to the British government.

4. PEC will announce further activities in coming issues of the *American Irish Newsletter.*

For further information contact
**AIEF-PEC, 54 South Liberty Drive
Suite 401, Stony Point, NY 10980, USA
(914) 947-2726. fax (914) 947-2599**

published August 1995 by AIEF-PEC

(*Reproduce & Distribute*)